JON HOTTEN

The Meaning of Cricket

Or,
How to Waste Your Life on an
Inconsequential Sport

YELLOW JERSEY PRESS
LONDON

1 3 5 7 9 10 8 6 4 2

Yellow Jersey Press
20 Vauxhall Bridge Road,
London SW1V 2SA

Yellow Jersey Press is part of the Penguin Random House group of companies
whose addresses can be found at global.penguinrandomhouse.com

Penguin
Random House
UK

First published in paperback by Yellow Jersey Press in 2017
First published in hardback by Yellow Jersey Press in 2016

penguin.co.uk/vintage

A CIP catalogue record for this book is available from the British Library

ISBN 9780224100199

Printed and bound by Clays Ltd, St Ives Plc

Penguin Random House is committed to a sustainable future
for our business, our readers and our planet. This book is made
from Forest Stewardship Council® certified paper

MIX
Paper from
responsible sources
FSC® C018179

To Mum and Dad, with love

'Cricket civilises people and creates good gentlemen'
                                        – Robert Mugabe

'With the bat, I was a soldier'

                                        – Viv Richards

Contents

I

The Miracle

The cricket coach Bob Woolmer once wrote: 'to review the raw, split-second data of what actually happens when a player executes a shot is to wonder how anyone survives more than one delivery.' Let's say it's the start of a game. You have taken guard in front of three stumps at one end of a cut strip that measures 22 yards in length. But that measure is from the set of stumps behind you to the set at the other end of the wicket. You are standing on the popping crease, 3ft in front of the stumps, and when the bowler delivers the ball his front foot will bisect the popping crease at his end, so in reality, there are less than 20 yards between him and you.

In your hands is a bat, made of English willow and with a rubber-spring cane handle spliced into it, the blade no more than 38in in length and 4¼in wide. It will weigh anywhere between 2lb 6oz and 3lb, heavier or lighter if you want it – the only limit here is the limit of the willow you can comfortably lift and manipulate.

The ball in the hands of your opponent has a wound cork core with four quarters of leather stitched around it, held in place by a raised seam. It weighs no less than 5½oz and no more than 5¾ and if it's new is still lacquered to a high shine. It is hard enough to break bones, to cause fatal injury when bowled or struck at speed onto a vulnerable area of the chest or head.

You are protected from the worst of the damage that the ball can inflict: pads, gloves, inner and outer thigh pads, box, perhaps a forearm guard and a chest pad, and always a helmet with a titanium grill. Although this kit is cumbersome, you will have worn it so often and for so long it will feel natural to make the moves you have to make, and after you've been hit on various parts of it a few times you will want the best available, because the ball has a habit of seeking out soft spots and weak points. The helmet is light and snug, but because the gap between the peak and the top of the grill needs to be narrow enough to prevent the ball from getting through should you be struck there, both remain within your peripheral vision. Nonetheless, there are large areas of your body which remain unprotected, and even those that are might not be safe. Justin Langer's one hundredth Test match ended after one ball when he was struck on the earpiece of his helmet by the South African opening bowler Makaya Ntini – in the hours afterwards, Langer, a black belt in karate renowned for being one of the toughest men in the game, endured a 'significant' concussion, weakness in his hands and arms and difficulty walking. The West Indian batsman Gordon Greenidge was once hit so violently in the groin that his box split in two and he vomited twice as he was being stretchered back to the dressing-rooms.*

None of this can enter your head as you wait for the bowler to begin his run. Instead, you must attempt to clear the mind of everything except for one conscious thought that will blot out the rest and switch the body on: 'watch the ball' being by far the most common. If you are a professional, or at least a serious amateur, you may have faced this bowler before and you will have some idea of what's coming, but on many occasions you will not. At any rate every match is different for any number of reasons and so you look for clues in the bowler's size, the length of his run, the position of the fielders.

As he comes in, it begins. You may want to watch the ball. You will probably be exhorting yourself to do so, either silently or in a whisper, but you will not do so, at least not in the way that you think you will.

For the first century or so of the game, no one understood what happened next. Science has only recently unpicked, in increments of milliseconds, what processes the body

*On 25 November 2014, Phillip Hughes, the Australian international who'd set a world record as the youngest player to score a century in both innings of a Test match, was struck in the neck by a short delivery while playing for South Australia against New South Wales in Sydney, and died in hospital from the injury two days later. The sadness felt throughout cricket was immediate and long-lasting. While the injury that he suffered was rare – the Australian team doctor noted only a hundred such cases ever reported and just one of those due to the impact of a cricket ball – Hughes' death was a raw and unwanted example of the danger inherent in the game.

goes through when confronted with a hard leather ball propelled towards it from close range, and why some people can deal with those brief fractions of time better than others.

The initial discovery, made decades ago, was that a batsman does not watch the ball right onto the bat. Photographs taken at the moment of impact showed that the eyes were more often than not shut, the head pointing in the direction the ball was expected to be hit. But it was not until detailed research by Land and McLeod in 2000 that the reality became clear, and the reality was this: however hard anyone willed themselves to look at the ball, they would do so only fleetingly. Instead, they would play a complex visual game with its flight. First, as the ball left the bowler's hand, the head would be still and watching. But then, about 140 milliseconds into the ball's journey, the eyes would shift rapidly downwards and away in a movement known as a saccade, to a point on the pitch where the brain anticipated that the ball would pitch. As the head followed the eyes downwards to that point, the eyes would move upwards again as the ball bounced to watch it for another 200 milliseconds until it moved ahead of the gaze for the final 100 milliseconds until impact.

Despite all of those hours of training and urging of the will, the eyes were on the ball for around 340 of the 600 milliseconds that it took to complete its journey – or, put more simply, 57 per cent of the time.

Peter Kirsten was one of the best South African players of the apartheid years, when the national side was prevented from competing in cricket beyond its boundaries. By the time the boycott was over and his country rejoined the international game Kirsten was 37, but still regarded as one of the finest players of fast bowling in the world. His first Test was against the West Indian battery of Patterson, Ambrose and Walsh in Barbados, and over the course of his career he faced almost all of the quickest bowlers on earth, including Allan Donald, Patrick Patterson, Devon Malcolm, Kapil Dev and Glenn McGrath.

In the early 1980s, a team of researchers at the University of Cape Town led by Tim Noakes asked Kirsten to take part in a simple experiment. With Kirsten batting in the nets, Noakes kept advancing the speed of a bowling machine until the ball was travelling too quickly for Kirsten to hit. Kirsten, who had faced hostile fast bowling of 95mph out in the middle, couldn't lay a bat on a delivery of 80mph when spat from the baleful eye of a static machine.

The experiment had demonstrated something basic and yet fundamental: even a player of Test match class relied on a series of clues from the bowler in order to be able to hit a ball travelling at more than 80mph. The long-standing notion that great batsmen have a better 'eye' than anyone else was clearly true, but more complex than first imagined.

Noakes then took things a stage further, linking the bowling machine to the lights at the indoor nets. The act of delivery triggered the switch, giving Kirsten the chance to see the first 100 to 200 milliseconds of the ball's flight before the room was thrown into darkness. Kirsten was still able to anticipate the length and direction of the delivery and get his bat on it. The experiment was then repeated with club cricketers. Few could hit the ball and some were so unnerved that they backed away entirely as the lights were extinguished.

It seemed certain, from this evidence, that great batsmen had an advantage: they were able to better predict the course of the ball early in its flight. The better the batsman, the more pronounced the gift. Bob Woolmer remembered a story told by Brian Lara, one of the most prodigiously talented batsmen in the history of the game. Lara was batting against England in Antigua in 1994. He was on the verge of breaking one of cricket's most famous and revered records, that of the highest score in a Test match, set in 1958 by Garry Sobers' innings of 365. After almost 12 hours at the crease, Lara had drawn level with Sobers. Chris Lewis was the bowler. Lara had not been able to score from the first two deliveries of Lewis' over, admitting that he was overcome by nerves. But as Lewis ran in for the third, Lara's fear disappeared. He knew long before Lewis actually bowled that the ball would be short, pitching halfway down the wicket. He was waiting for it, and cracked it away for the runs that brought him the record.

That ability to pick up cues, both as the bowler approached the crease and then delivered the ball, seemed to be the secret at the heart of batsmanship. The greatest players could see and interpret them better than anyone else.* As Bob Woolmer said, without that understanding

*Events in baseball have confirmed the notion. In his book *The Sports Gene*, David Epstein cites the example of numerous big-league sluggers who were unable to lay bat on a ball purveyed by Jennie Finch, the world's leading female softball pitcher. Although Finch's pitches were around ten miles an hour slower than those in Major League baseball, she delivered them underhand, and after a lifetime building up visual clues given by overarm pitchers, their brains could not adapt quickly enough to the unfamiliar angle of delivery.

the fact that a batsman could hit a single ball would seem like a miracle.

In the course of his record-breaking innings of 375 in Antigua, Lara faced 538 balls. Two months later, with his gifts approaching their peak, he made the highest first-class score, an innings of 501 not out for Warwickshire against Durham at Edgbaston. Astonishingly, a decade on, after Matthew Hayden had surpassed Lara's Test record with a score of 380 against a barely international-class Zimbabwe team, Lara reclaimed it by making 400 not out, again against England and again on the same ground, St John's in Antigua. Lara's talent was not only rare, it was enduring.

In all, he faced 19,753 balls in Test match cricket and another 13,086 in one-day internationals before he retired in 2007. Only 483 of those resulted in his dismissal, so 32,356 did not. Put differently, just 1.47 per cent of the deliveries bowled at Brian Lara got him out.

Bob Woolmer did the first amazing thing I ever saw on a cricket field. It was August 1976, at the Kennington Oval. England were playing West Indies, fifth Test, second day. Viv Richards was 200 not out overnight. The Oval outfield had been turned brown by a six-week heatwave that showed no signs of abating. The ground was sold out. Most of the crowd seemed to be supporting West Indies. My father bought us seat cushions from a man who had hundreds of them piled up on a trolley, and when we got to our seats I saw why: it was just a thin wooden bench. It was close to the pitch, though, and I could reach out and put my hands on the perimeter hoardings. The players came out just before 11.30 under a raking sun. Richards casually defended a few balls and then hit one off his legs through midwicket, firmly but not hard enough to reach the boundary. All Bob Woolmer did was run after it and throw it back in. He picked it up well inside the rope and fielded it in the way he had done hundreds of times before and would do hundreds of times again. It was utterly routine, except I'd never seen a ball thrown that far in my life. It flew in a low arc hard into Alan Knott's gloves, its severity completely at odds with the effort, or, rather, lack of it, that Woolmer seemed to impart.

In the 1970s, English cricketers did not look like gods. They did not look like athletes. Some of them didn't even look like cricketers. Bob Woolmer could have stepped from an illustration of a schoolboy in a 1950s comic: pudgy hands, chubby cheeks, a slight paunch, but with a general air of well-fed vigour. The England captain Tony Greig's nearest physical equivalent was John Cleese; when Greig approached the crease to bowl, he wasn't so much running as unfolding like a seaside deckchair. David Steele, who batted at number three, wore thick glasses and had grey hair. Derek Underwood, a freakish spinner who bowled at almost medium-pace, had the look of a distracted Oxford don; a severe forehead with a few combed-over strands and a gentle, flat-footed run.

The difference between England and West Indies was best illustrated by their nicknames. Where David Steele was known as 'the bank clerk who went to war', Viv Richards had the moniker 'Smokey', because his muscly,

triangular frame could have belonged to the boxer Smokin'
Joe Frazier. England's opening bowler, Bob Willis, was
called 'Goose' because he looked like one when he ran
in. West Indies opening bowler, Michael Holding, was
called 'Whispering Death' because he approached so ath-
letically and from so far away that the umpire couldn't
hear him coming. Their skipper, Clive Lloyd, was known
as 'Cat' after the way he swooped down on the ball from
cover.

West Indies were already the masters of a new game,
one-day internationals, at which they had won the first
World Cup the summer before at Lord's. Now, Lloyd
was constructing a war machine that would change Test
match cricket forever: four brutal fast bowlers, seven
attacking batsmen. To a traditional game of skill they
brought a fearsome physicality; they made the ball go
faster, harder, further than ever before, whether bowling,
batting or fielding. In the World Cup final, Viv Richards
had thrown down the stumps twice from backward
square leg and run out another at the bowler's end. Then
he had embarked on a year of Test batting that would lay
waste to all of the history that had come before it. Since
New Year's Day, against Australia, India and England, he
had made 44, 2, 30, 101, 50, 98, 142, 130, 20, 177, 23, 64,
232, 63, 4, 135, 66 and 38. Now, at The Oval in his last
innings of 1976, he went from 200 not out overnight to
291. He was bowled by Tony Greig just as the ground had
begun to consider the possibility that he might challenge
Sobers' 365.

Lloyd declared at 5.30pm with the score at 687, more
than West Indies had ever made in England before. Bob

Woolmer and Dennis Amiss, England's openers, had half an hour to bat. When it became obvious that Lloyd was going to declare, the men sitting behind us had begun to argue over the pair of binoculars that they were sharing. 'I'm having the first over of Amiss,' one said. No one seemed to think that Dennis could survive many more. It would be brief but spectacular. He had an odd stance where he turned his chest towards the bowler, yet despite the barracking of the crowd, who were all pretty drunk, and the heat, which had accumulated not just through the day but through that endless summer, and the speed of Andy Roberts and Michael Holding, who sent the ball down so quickly it was all but invisible from 80 yards away, Amiss and Woolmer survived the night.

Bob Woolmer was out to Holding early the next morning. Many years later he gave this description of the experience: 'Holding's feet hardly touched the ground as he ran in. He moved in silkily and his body swayed like a cobra's: it would have been magnificent had I been watching from the outside. But here I was more intent on watching the ball, moving back and across as Colin Cowdrey had taught me.

'Holding was bowling with only one fielder in front of wicket at cover-point. He bowled, and I moved back and across. I saw that the ball was pitched up, so I moved forward, feet first, and then into the shot.

'Before I knew it, the ball had smashed into my pad. Even though I was wearing state-of-the-art buckskin pads, the pain was so incredible that I thought I had been shot. A small explosion of whitening emanated from my pad and a loud appeal from the bowler and the fielders.

Dickie Bird was not known to give too many lbws. But this time he had no choice: the ball would have broken the middle stump.'

To survive a single delivery propelled at almost one hundred miles an hour took the body and brain to the edges of their capabilities. Woolmer had resisted Holding while Holding made a series of small errors in length and line, yet Woolmer's first mistake dismissed him, excluded him from further participation. It was the same for any batsman, however great, however needy.

Yet here lay the genius of the game, and it was this: one chance. One chance was the key to it all. Anyone who ever walked to the crease and took guard, from Bradman who averaged 99.94 to New Zealand's famous number 11 Chris Martin, who got to double figures once in 94 Test match innings, had the same. One chance, one mistake, one umpire's error.

It was a cruel, illuminating beauty, and from its beginnings no batsman has been immune from its iniquities. The intrinsic unfairness of it had led men to indignation, delusion, self-righteousness, despair, depression and worse.

Cricket's first superstar was also the first to fall prey to this state of mind. William Gilbert Grace was notorious for standing his ground, daring the umpire (or anyone else) to give him out. At a match at Leyton in 1898, the good doctor was engaged in battle with Essex's Charles Kortright, the fastest bowler in the land, who tore into him, driving Grace back with short balls before having him caught behind and plumb lbw in the course of one over. Dander up, Grace growled and glared at the umpire, daring him to raise his finger. Cowed by the most famous man in Victorian England, he didn't. Kortright roared in once more, ripping one through Grace and removing two stumps from the ground. WG held the crease for a second longer before turning and stomping off, his mood as dark as his beard.

'Going already, Doctor?' Kortright said. 'There's still one stump standing.'

Cricket is unique among sports in its psychological aspect. It's a team game, but there is no other team game so dependent on individual performance: indeed, at any moment, almost 90 per cent of one side is not taking part. A football match might turn on a fraction of a second, but even a striker missing an open goal knows he may get another opportunity. A baseball might be harder to hit, but a slugger gets three chances before being dismissed, and nine innings in a game. Cricket is perhaps most like golf in its duration, its mental challenge and its need for fine motor skills, but the golfer is striking a stationary ball. In its combination of time, opportunity and the constant threat of disaster, cricket is exquisitely balanced and uniquely able to drive its participants to despair. It is a game with a high incidence of suicide among its players. The writer David Frith found more than a hundred for his moving book *Silence of the Heart*. The suicide rate among Test match cricketers of all nationalities is 2.07 per cent, compared to an average of 1.07 in the general population. As Frith writes, 'cricket is stuck with its dreadful burden'. What causes it? Perhaps it attracts more introverted people. I am one. Yet it is impossible to generalise: some of cricket's suicides have been from players unable to bear their departure from the warm insularity of its dressing-room environment.

For others it is the absence of the act itself. Geoffrey Boycott admitted that it was too painful for him to pick up a bat once he had retired: he couldn't control the emotions that flooded through him when he did. One of his former team-mates, Derek Randall, was the opposite, finding solace in Minor Counties cricket. Many club players have a story about stumbling across a former pro enjoying the uncomplicated pleasures of the amateur game. Others write about it, analyse it, talk about it on television and radio, photograph it, stand as umpires, join committees, give after-dinner talks. Jack Russell, the former England wicketkeeper, paints it. Few, in my experience, can leave it alone. It is a game that is defined by its statistics, and yet it has a vast internal hinterland that is unmapped, and experienced differently by everyone who travels there. Cricket, in its essential strangeness, does things to you.

In a game at The Oval in 1870, a Surrey batsman called James Southerton hit a ball violently into the ground from where it flew up into the hands of W. G. Grace, who was fielding at cover for MCC. So obvious had been the bounce of the ball that there was no appeal, but perhaps because of the celebrity of the fielder Southerton walked off to the pavilion and could not be persuaded to return. Who knows what was in his mind? Faced with this unparalleled situation, the scorer recorded Southerton as 'Retired, thinking he was out'.

Grace himself had to be detonated from the crease ('going already, Doctor?'); Southerton went when he didn't have to. These parts of the cricketing psyche, opposite sides of the same heightened state, have travelled across centuries and remain deeply understood by everyone who has played the game.

'Thinking he was out'.

This is what it does. This is how it starts.

2
Harold, Alf and Me

Harold Pinter called cricket 'God's greatest creation'. In 2005, ailing and swaddled under a checked blanket, the new Laureate delivered in his Nobel Lecture a withering dismissal of the United States government and its foreign policy, yet he was too shy to have ever contemplated meeting the great Yorkshire batsman Len Hutton, his all-time hero.

Pinter once wrote a poem about Hutton. In full, it ran:

> *I saw Len Hutton in his prime,*
> *Another time, another time.*

He sent it to his friend the playwright Simon Gray, and then rang the following day to ask him what he thought.

'I haven't finished it yet,' Gray said.

Above Pinter's writing desk he had a painting of himself batting in the nets, given to him by his club, the Gaieties. Soon after he died, I saw a photograph of it in the paper. I didn't immediately recognise Pinter, who looks young and hawkish, but I knew the net that he was batting in instantly; it was as familiar to me as any house I've ever lived in. It was the Gover Cricket School in Wandsworth, south London, and, what's more, the stumps in the painting were the wrong colour, brown where they should have been grey, as was the flooring – although in reality that was so indeterminate in nature, a kind of mismatched rubberised lino that I've never seen anywhere else before or since, Michelangelo would have struggled to capture its essence.

The school was halfway up East Hill, set back from the road behind an old garage forecourt. Bill Brooke had established it in 1928 with a couple of Surrey and England players, Herbert Strudwick and the great Andy Sandham, who was the first Englishman to make a Test match triple-century – 325 against West Indies in Jamaica. Alf Gover played for Surrey and England too, and he married Bill Brooke's daughter Marjorie in 1932. Alf bought Strudwick's share of the school in 1938 and then Sandham's just after the war and soon the school bore his name. He and Marjorie lived in the rather grand house next door, from where Marjorie looked after the finances. By the time I first went, in the winter in which I turned 13 years old, the school was probably the most famous coaching establishment in the country. Among those to have passed through its narrow side door were Viv Richards, Andy Roberts, Colin Cowdrey, Barry Richards, Garry Sobers, Frank Tyson, Ken Barrington, Tom Graveney, Sunil Gavaskar and Rohan Kanhai. Long after I had left, Brian Lara went there, too. Then there was Pinter and Trevor McDonald and John Major, none of them cricketers, but all happily obsessed with both the game and with this place. But the whole point of Alf's was that anyone could go: all you needed was the price of a half-hour's coaching, which when I began was four pounds, settled up afterwards in Alf's office. All human life was there.

As I sat in front of my screen staring at Harold Pinter's painting, everything about it came back with an almost overwhelming force, an extraordinary sense-memory of how it looked, felt and smelled (that *smell* – eggy, gassy, unforgettable). The frontage was relatively new and whitewashed, but the school itself was located in an industrial shed attached to the back. Once you'd turned your bag sideways to get it through that slender side door and climbed the wobbly stairs that opened out onto a snooker room and a small bar, both dimly, effortfully lit by yellowing bulbs, it was like entering the land that time forgot. The place was probably unchanged from the day it had opened, save for the addition of a big colour TV at the back of the snooker room, which was usually tuned to horse racing or rugby matches.

Up another thin, dark corridor beyond the snooker room was the dressing-room, small and damp, the final frontier before the journey through a tiny, cold passage that led to the nets. It was impossible to cross that boundary without thinking of everyone who had done so before, and feeling their weight – this intangible sensation, I would learn, was true of all of cricket's great places.

And those nets . . . Pushing through the heavy canvas that covered the entrance could be perilous if mistimed: it opened onto the middle two lanes and a straight drive walloped at the wrong moment might come screaming at you. It was like nowhere else. The roof, supported by triangular steel rafters that would clang and vibrate like dampened bells when a ball struck them, was low, the air still and cool, the building unheated and lit by gas lamps because Alf had never got round to having electricity installed. The hall itself was probably 25 yards long, so once some space behind the stumps at the batsman's end and the briefest of run-ups for the bowlers – four or five strides – was allowed for, the combatants were no more than 18 yards apart. The surroundings had the effect of amplifying what was going on. Sometimes a big player, a *real* player, would pass through. I often saw Surrey's mighty middle-order hitter Monte Lynch practise with a silent fury, ball after ball thudding into the canvas. It was like watching a heavyweight boxer working on the bag. And I once stood at the back of a lane while a future West Indies batsman called Carlisle Best laid waste to the place. When things like that happened it could be like being inside a drum, the air thrumming with the sheer proximity of such force.

Among it all was Alf himself, who was in his seventies by then – well, sort of. He'd been born on a leap year day, so he was still technically somewhere in his teens. I must have seen him hundreds of times over the winters I went, and he was always dressed identically: immaculate cream flannels, a white cravat under his stiff collar, silver hair swept nobly back and, most impressively, his England sweater, three lions in its centre, now so long it almost reached his knees. Sometimes, in his office, which was behind the snooker room, he would wear a blue England blazer, too.

Alf still coached and would bowl for half an hour from a standing position, lobbing the ball down with an almost horizontal arm, his shoulder brought low by 1,555 first-class wickets – eight of those in Tests – and a lifetime of cricket. In retrospect it was like facing a very slow version of Lasith Malinga. He was once coaching a young bowler and was urging him to bring his arm up higher in his action. 'No, like this . . .' said Alf in increasingly frustrated tones, the kid copying him perfectly.

It was a tradition at the school that any new arrival's first lesson would be with Alf, whereupon he would offer a gentle judgement of prospects, euphemistically couched: 'He'll get a lot of enjoyment from the game . . .' I don't remember what he said about me after my first lesson, but it was evidently enough to keep going with. My dad was the engine behind that, working all week and then driving us the 35 miles there and 35 miles back for a half-hour lesson that I suspect was for him not inexpensive. He had such belief in my game that, had Alf told him I had more chance of becoming lead dancer at the Royal Ballet than a decent cricketer, he would have disregarded it as the opinion of a layman.

It may appear impossibly hit or miss to identify a player at an early age. There are, at any moment, thousands of gainfully employed professional cricketers and thousands more who have retired. Weight of numbers suggests that they can't all have a common experience growing up. Yet because cricket is a game primarily of skill rather than strength, it does lend itself to prodigies. Almost every pro who makes it as far as the ghosted autobiography recounts there an early feat or two that marked them out. Then there are the true marvels. Cricket's highest ever individual score is 628 not out, made by a 13-year-old called A. E. J. Collins over four consecutive afternoons in June 1899 at Clifton College near Bristol. The game, between two houses at the school, was timeless and played on a square ground with three short boundaries that counted only two for hitting them, and another longer side where hits had to be all-run. By the fourth afternoon, word had spread across the country, and the match was being covered by *The Times*. As Collins ran out of partners, the Thunderer reported with a hint of disapproval that he hit 'recklessly' and was 'dropped with his score on 605 and 619'. 'He has a reputation as great as the most advertised soap: he will be immortalised,' wrote a cheerier journalist, and so it has proved. Collins died at Ypres in 1914 aged 29, along with two of his brothers.*

W. G. Grace, who would grow up to score 13 hundreds on the cricket ground at Clifton and later sent his sons to the College, appeared against the Clifton town team for

---

*In January 2015, a 15-year-old rickshaw driver's son, Pranav Dhanawade, scored 1,009 not out from 323 deliveries in a match for K. C. Gandhi School against Arya Gurukul School during a cup match in Kalyan, a town 40 kilometres outside Mumbai. The innings received blanket media coverage in India and Pranav was congratulated by Sachin Tendulkar and M. S. Dhoni via Twitter. Soon afterwards an investigation by the *Indian Express* newspaper cast some doubt on its legitimacy: although Pranav was 15, most of the Arya Gurukal side were much younger, the stars of their usual XI having been stopped from playing by the school's principal. Two of the four bowlers were Under-12 cricketers and had never played on a full-sized pitch, or with a full-sized ball or bowled more than nine overs in a game. Their coach's hope was that they would get the ball to the other end 'without it bouncing twice'. The groundsman at the Wayle Maidan, on which the game was played, said the pitch was unsuitable for even Under-14 cricketers as the boundaries on either side were not much more than 30 yards. K. C. Gandhi declared on 1,465-3 and won by an innings and 1,382 runs.

West Gloucester when he was 11 years old and made 51. Don Bradman scored his first century at the age of 12, was undefeated on 37 in his debut match against adults and then left cricket and played tennis for two years. In 1925–6, aged 17, he returned in a cup match for Bowral against Wingello, who had the future Test bowler Bill O'Reilly in their team. On a matting wicket, he scored 234. Perhaps not surprisingly Bowral reached the finals of the competition, where Bradman made 320 not out in a match that extended across five Saturdays. The following year he played on a grass wicket for the first time ever, in the Sydney Grade competition, and scored 110.

Sachin Tendulkar, the batsman who would come to remind Bradman most of himself, was perhaps the most prodigious schoolboy cricketer of all time. As a 13-year-old, not much more than 5ft tall and playing in Under-15 schools competitions for Shardashram Vidyamandir, he made seven centuries and two double-centuries in a single summer. The following season he was named in Bombay's first-class squad for the first time, and the season after that, still just 15, he began with scores of 130, 107, 117 and 175 in various age group events. Then came, consecutively, 21 not out, 125, 207 not out, 329 not out and 346 not out. The first of those triple-centuries was made alongside his childhood friend Vinod Kambli, a left-hander who himself scored 348 not out in a world record partnership of 664, a stand that quickly became famous across India. The next time Tendulkar batted, Mumbai's Maidan was flooded with people. Unbowed by the pressure, he ended the first day of the match unbeaten on 122, the second on 286 and by the lunchtime declaration on day three had made 346 to take his average past a thousand. He then bowled the first ball of the opposition innings. Tendulkar duly became one of the ten players in history to make their Test debut aged 16. A generation later, as Tendulkar's son Arjun began to make his way in the game, one of his club-mates at MIG, a 14-year-old called Prithvi Shaw, scored 546 in a Harris Shield match. With a heavy sense of portent, the innings concluded four days after Tendulkar made the last of his 200 Test match appearances for India.

Such prodigiousness is no guarantee. Of the other nine players to debut in Tests as 16-year-olds, only two, Pakistan batsman Mushtaq Mohammad and Bangladesh wicketkeeper Mushfiqur Rahim, have had international careers of any note.

Peter Roebuck played for Somerset seconds when he was 13 years old and 4ft 2in tall. Roebuck would later write brilliantly about the ambiguity of his ambition as a cricketer, and never quite got as far as people thought he might.

Wisden called another Somerset batsman, Mark Lathwell, 'a major discovery . . . not since David Gower has a young player quickened the pulse like Lathwell'. With Graham Gooch's England captaincy in its last days of Rome phase, he was called into the team at 21 having made 175 for the England A team against Tasmania. He played twice, scored 20, 0, 33 and 25 and was dropped. He lost his confidence and then his love for it all, and drifted out of the game before he was 30, his name raised every time the notion of lost promise was discussed. 'I knew deep down that I wasn't quite ready,' he said later. 'At least I didn't let myself be taken in, because I honestly did think it would probably come crashing down. Which it did.'

Perhaps no player in history has seen his promise disintegrate as spectacularly as Vinod Kambli, Sachin Tendulkar's friend and partner in that stand of 664. As the shockwaves from the game spread along the city's cricket-obsessed streets, there didn't seem to be much to choose between the two players. While Sachin was the more studious and apparently the hungrier for runs, Kambli, a classically freewheeling left-hander, was flashier and more exciting to watch.

Tendulkar was the first to advance. His Test debut could not have been harder, made in 1989 in the white heat of Karachi against Pakistan amidst the fiercest rivalry in cricket. He was struck on the head during his first innings. In his second he made 50. The following summer in England he scored his first Test century, and four months after that, on tour in Australia, got 148 not out at the Sydney Cricket Ground and then 114 in Perth on the lightning-quick glass of the WACA, an instant classic of an innings that was acclaimed as one of the greatest ever played in Australia.

It took Kambli a while to catch up with his school friend. By the time he made his Test debut, against England in Kolkata at the end of January 1993, Tendulkar had 21 caps and was already regarded as the best young batsman in the game. 'It was as if Sachin took the elevator while I took the stairs,' Kambli said, a comment that some interpreted as a jibe at India's baroque caste system – Tendulkar was a loftier Brahmin, which had long provided most of India's players, Kambli a Dalit, just the second ever from an 'untouchable' caste to play for the national side. Kambli sometimes found himself abused by the crowds, not that it affected his swagger. On his debut for Mumbai against Gujarat in the Ranji Trophy, he'd hit his first delivery for six. For the Test side his impact was even more devastating. Kambli's first eight innings, which came against England, Zimbabwe and Sri Lanka, went: 16, 18 not out, 59, 224, 227, 125, 4, 120. It had taken Tendulkar 14 innings to make his maiden hundred, and he would not record a double-century until he'd been playing Test cricket for a decade. Kambli had two in his first five innings. After seven Test matches he had 793 runs at 113.28. Only five batsmen in history – Bradman, Headley, Worrell, Weekes and Gavaskar – had done better. What was just as remarkable was the fashion in which he scored them. Kambli had learned to bat on a tiny inner-city pitch surrounded by tall buildings and the higher a player could hit the ball into them the more runs he was awarded. Kambli carved bowlers everywhere, and was particularly severe on spin. When he came to play against Australia in an ODI, he hit Shane Warne for 22 in a single over. His louche technique was at odds with the orthodoxy of Test cricket in the early 1990s, and an unnamed England bowler was heard to say that he could 'knock Kambli over with an orange . . .'

'Better get that orange soon,' one of his team-mates muttered as Kambli smashed them to all parts of the Wankhede Stadium.

Kambli was, in retrospect, an avatar of the India soon to emerge, new, free, modern; hungry for what the coming years held and eager to shape them. Yet he was also, as the boxing trainer Teddy Atlas once said of Mike Tyson, 'a comet not a star'. In a country where batsmen are worshipped and obsessed over, Kambli, the low-caste kid, began wearing gold earrings and flashy chains. While Tendulkar retained an ascetic devotion to the art of bats-manship, Kambli simply went for everything that life was suddenly offering him. He finished the series against Sri Lanka well, with scores of 82 in Bangalore and 57 in Ahmedabad, but then it began, his precipitous fall. India's newest sensation would bat just ten more times in Test cricket. Against New Zealand in Hamilton he made 9 and 19. Against West Indies in Mumbai, Nagpur and Mohali, he scored 40, 0, 0, 6, 18, 0, and against New Zealand in Bangalore and Cuttack 27 and 28. He kept slashing the ball to the slips and gully. It got into his head. He began to look for reasons. He ended up with nine rubber grips on his bat handle. He obsessed over its size and feel.

He was still just 24 and his batting average stood at 54.20. It seems impossible that he'd never be chosen again, never get another chance, but he wasn't and he didn't. Over the next five years he was dropped and recalled at least nine times to India's one-day team, where his fra-gility against the short ball outside off stump was less exposed. He began to drift, a marooned enigma, his fail-ings given even starker relief by Tendulkar's unending success. As his friend became first a legend and then a god, rich beyond dreams and so desperate for escape that his favourite pastime was to drive undisturbed at 3am on Mumbai's deserted freeways, Kambli became a joke, his name scorned. He tried to get into Bollywood. He stood for political office. He married, divorced, remarried. He converted to Christianity. He claimed on a reality TV show that Sachin could have done more to help him. In November 2013, a fortnight after Tendulkar had played his 200th and final Test and retired in glory, he suffered a heart attack while driving and required emergency surgery to save his life.

What happened to Vinod Kambli was strange and sad, his career linked forever to Tendulkar's and forever overshadowed by it, a cautionary tale on the nature of promise and its outcomes.

My first memory of cricket is probably unreliable, an amalgam of sensory flashbacks from different moments, but I'm in the kitchen at home with my first proper bat, a Stuart Surridge that cost four quid from the sports shop in Fleet and that I could barely lift. The song playing on the radio is 'Rhinestone Cowboy', which must mean it's the summer of 1975. I am ten years old. My dad had carefully applied two coats of linseed oil to the bat, bringing out the grain of the wood. Bats are no longer oiled but even the faintest trace of the smell of linseed transports me to that bat and that moment; the same with the leather of my batting gloves. Before I ever went near a cricket club, or Alf Gover's school, I batted for hours in the back garden against my father's bowling. He was of the view that true batsmanship was about off-side play, so the wicket ran alongside our neighbour's fence to prevent leg-side slogs. My obsession slowly dragged the rest of the family in. My sister, younger by two years, had her own cutdown bat that she regularly hurled over that leg-side fence on dismissal (she has the volcanic sporting temperament that I wished I'd had too) and my mum bowled loopy, cunning underarm and fielded in an old pair of batting gloves. For some reason she always adopted a cricketing

26

persona when she played and for a long time she was the wily, wiry Indian spinner Bishan Bedi, before an unlikely shift one summer to the somewhat obscure West Indian middle-order batsman Faoud Bacchus.

Geoffrey Boycott's *Book for Young Cricketers* recommended suspending an old ball from a string – I had one hanging from the tree by the shed. Around it I created an alternative universe. Practising on it always began the same way, with a walk down the patio steps and out to the tree to open the batting for England. I was usually accompanied by my cricketing hero, Barry Richards, who technically was South African, but as they were banned from playing Test match cricket for reasons I didn't really understand, my England were now selecting him. It hardly drew a murmur from the commentators in my head because they spent almost all of their time discussing the reasons why a ten-year-old was good enough to play Test cricket. Their doubts were dispelled as soon as Richards and myself set about the bowling attacks of the world. Barry usually outscored me early, but by lunch I was hitting my stride and drawing level with a trademark fusillade of boundaries. I carefully measured out each session of play via the number of swings the ball took from the tree. If Richards went early, I often forged a long partnership with David Steele, the obdurate and bespectacled Northamptonshire number three who'd spent much of the actual Test match summer of 1975 defying Thomson and Lillee as a part of Tony Greig's Ashes side ('who have we got here, Groucho Marx?' Thomson said when Steele marched out to bat against him for the first time). Sometimes my England would collapse and I'd eke out runs with the tail, and on other, rarer occasions, I would be dismissed early in the first innings, maybe for nought, and the commentators would talk harshly about the folly of having a ten-year-old in the side, but in the second innings would come the inevitable century, often match-winning, and the commentators would have to admit that the selectors had been right all along.

Cricket's place in my internal life had solidified early, and I discovered that I was far from alone. I was given a copy of a Lord's Taverners' book which had an essay by Christopher Martin-Jenkins in which he described his childhood 'Tests'. He was not only the star player, he'd invented an entire population around him, full teams for England and the other nations, each with their own biographies and stats. He even held imaginary selection meetings that featured dramatic arguments over who should play. During my time in the game, I've met at least two adult players who admit that they still commentate on themselves in their heads during matches.

My love for cricket then was simple and ardent and richly fed. My dad's seemed more mysterious in origin. How had he found it? He was born in Hackney in 1927. Hackney is gentrified now but it wasn't then. I only went to the house he grew up in a couple of times before it was condemned, but I remember how forbidding it seemed. It was dark and cold. The rooms were as small as cupboards. It still had an outside toilet. The only heat came from the fireplace. Every house in the street was the same. My grandparents, my dad and his three sisters had all lived in that house, the boundaries of their universe drawn in tightly around them. He left school at 12. He'd had a teacher who would let them play cricket during breaks, and would put a penny coin on his stumps for anyone who could hit them. But then the war began. He stayed in London throughout. His mum didn't want her children evacuated, and the war went on long enough for him to be called up just as it ended. He did a few months in the navy before the officers, now desperate to clear everyone out, told him to say he had claustrophobia and he was demobbed. Cricket was nowhere, but he became an excellent table tennis player and somehow managed to join a tennis club, where he met my mother. They were adventurers. They took a ship around the world, getting off in New Zealand and staying for a year. They came home via America. One day he was driving through Hampshire for work and saw a brand new house set back from the road in a town he'd never heard of and bought it. His family thought he was mad for leaving London. They thought he was mad for buying a house. They did it anyway, and instead of a grim two-up, two-down council place in Hackney, my sister and I grew up in a new bungalow with trees in the garden and a lawn that acted as cricket and football pitch, a tennis and badminton court, even the odd golf hole. He'd barely been to a cricket match. The only one he can remember was a trip to The Oval, where by magnificent chance he saw Bradman's final innings, but somehow he magicked up tickets for us: that unforgettable day at The Oval for Richards' 291 being the first; a day at the Centenary Test at Lord's when Australia's opener Graham Wood made a hundred (I still have the first-day cover we mailed back from the ground); and, even more remarkably, tickets for the 1979 and 1983

World Cup finals. He put cricket at the centre of our lives and it became something that we have always shared; a fall-back position. On the few occasions in my life when we have argued – almost always prompted by something idiotic I'd done – we would begin to reconcile by talking about cricket. Even now, he is the bowler I have faced more than any other. He was never quick and didn't do much with the ball but he was remorselessly accurate and his action is as familiar to me as the back of my hand. He had a short approach and a little hitch in his penultimate step, but his delivery stride was long and he had a full turn of the shoulders that, with the wide, low swing of his bowling arm, was endlessly repeatable and enabled him to land the ball where he wanted. In the summer he would get up at six, drink two cups of tea and smoke a couple of roll-ups, drive an hour to work, get home at six, have dinner and then have to bowl at me, sometimes cutting the grass beforehand, too. I was nothing but impatient for it: 'can we play cricket tonight?' I'd ask before he was even fully out of the car. Often we'd be out there until nine o'clock and if he yearned for winter he never showed it. And then, in the winters, came Alf's.

The prodigy is isolated by talent. That wasn't a problem that I appeared to have. At the end of my first season, my highest score was 22. I was beginning to discover the implications of 'one chance', cricket's psychological pivot-point. When I batted in the nets at Alf's or in the back garden with my dad, all I thought about was where I was going to hit the ball. Getting out didn't enter my mind. In a match it was all I thought of. The nerves and the fear of disappointment – for myself, for my dad, who'd become deeply invested in every innings – were overwhelming and inhibiting. I was being introduced to the game's strange and tantalising allure, to begin every innings in failure . . . In the certain life of a secure and happy child, it introduced the first notes of uncertainty from the real world.

Cricket, and Alf's, was beginning to let parts of that real world in, too, a world of grown men. My coach for several years was, in complete contrast to the patrician and noble Alf, an Australian named Jim Cameron. Jim was a buccaneering, quixotic and enigmatic figure, red-headed and bearded, fiery and wise. He was sometimes in the company of impossibly glamorous women who seemed to be in his thrall and he often looked like he'd been up all night, which he probably had. Jim taught me how to bat, properly bat, and he toughened me up. There were no helmets then, and no health and safety either, not that Jim would have taken much notice of either. Once, trying to make a point about something or other, he came and stood right in front of me, about three feet away, and told me to hit the ball at him as hard as I could. I did, and he caught it easily. He'd spent so many hours bowling in the nets at Alf's that he could send down almost anything from a new ball peppering to all kinds of weird, wristy spins.

He sometimes made jokes that I didn't really understand but thought that I should laugh at. My dad, who rarely went out (after working, getting in and playing cricket with me, I can't blame him, and he's always been teetotal) arranged a night with Jim that ended up at my dad's friend Wally's snooker club. By the time my dad left in the early hours, Jim was by all accounts just getting warmed up. He and my dad sometimes alluded to what may have happened – laughs, raised eyebrows – but it was a weird, alien world into which I was yet to be inducted.

After the last coaching session of the day Jim was often behind the bar at Alf's serving drinks. All kinds of people met in that bar. I never saw Harold Pinter, but Timothy West, the actor, took his son along and Jim and the other coaches brought in all sorts, most of whom engaged in long snooker matches on Alf's pay-as-you-go table; Alf would, very occasionally and if the bar was quiet, tell some stories, too. I remember one about the time he was nightwatchman at The Oval for Surrey, and somehow – he was a proper number 11 – survived long into the next morning, until his partner walked down the wicket and told him it was about time he got out. His partner was Percy Fender. His captain was *Douglas Jardine*. Alf once opened the bowling for MCC in India, and, in the grip of the dreaded belly, simply ran past the stumps without delivering the ball, straight up the pavilion steps and into the toilet. 'Lost by a few yards,' he used to say.

Cricket's greatest player did not play enough to be called a prodigy. In fact Bradman probably played less cricket at a young age than anyone who has gone on to greatness in the game. In him is one of cricket's greatest mysteries, one of sport's greatest mysteries: why was Bradman so good? His immortal Test match batting average of 99.94 makes him statistically almost 40 per cent better than anyone else to have played the game. Usain Bolt would have to run the 100m in seven seconds to dominate his event in the same way. Tiger Woods would need to win another ten major championships, Roger Federer another five. What Bradman did on a cricket field has proved unattainable to anyone else in any sport, and yet in his solitary childhood in his country town he played very little formal cricket and was never coached. It would be easy in those circumstances to dismiss him as a freak, an outlier, a cosmic fluke who happened to descend on cricket in a particular time and place. Trying to explain Bradman would be like trying to explain Shakespeare or Mozart – they had the same 26 letters or 12 notes as everyone else; they just knew how to use them better.

The era of Bradman's birth is important. An only child living in an Australian country town during the First World War, he had to make his own entertainment. Bradman's consisted of a game. It was played in the outdoor porch, which housed a water tank with a corrugated metal jacket. Bradman would stand about eight feet away from the tank in front of a wooden door that served as a wicket – or at least as something to protect. Using a cricket stump, he would strike a golf ball against the horizontal ridges of the tank and then hit the return as it flew back towards him at unpredictable angles. For day after day Bradman struck the tiny, hard golf ball with the rounded stump, a remarkable feat of hand–eye co-ordination performed unconsciously. There is a very short black and white cine-film shot with Bradman as an adult demonstrating the game, the only existing clue that we have into his early development as a sportsman. In it, he hits the ball repeatedly against the tank, the slim stump moving in a constant motion in response to the odd angles that the bounce produces. The ball is a blur, almost invisible as it flies back and forth. 'In this way,' he said, 'I developed a sense of distance and pace.'

Jeff Thomson tells a story about Bradman attending an Australian training session during the tour of India in 1977–8, when the Don was 68 and hadn't picked up a bat for 20 years. Bradman strode into the net wearing no pads and proceeded to, in Thomson's words, 'belt hell' out of a pair of local net bowlers. Thomson decided to bowl some leg-spin and Bradman hit that, too. 'I went back in [to the dressing-room],' Thomson recalled, 'and said, why isn't this bastard playing tomorrow? That's how good he was.'

Bradman fulfils any theory of development subscribed to him: genetic suitability; Gladwell's 10,000 hours of practice; and as soon as he began playing formal cricket he was scoring runs in unprecedented volume and did so throughout his career. Even bodyline, that strange and devastating manifestation of empirical suppression which was designed specifically to stop him and almost destroyed the game in the process, merely – and briefly – brought his returns down to a level that only 12 other players have ever matched.

There it was and there it stands, 99.94, a figure that will never be approached, set by an unfathomable genius, the most prodigious of them all. The scale of Bradman's achievement has tended to ward off any study of how he did what he did. After all, that would be like trying to unpick Shakespeare by parsing his sentences or going through Mozart with a chord chart. And yet Bradman's childhood game may contain an answer. Its legacy was the foundation of his batting technique, which was deeply unconventional. The way that Bradman gripped the bat and the way he took his stance closed the bat face so that the leading edge was pointing at the bowler as he ran in. From this position, Bradman picked the bat up at an angle towards gully and swung in an inverted arc towards the ball, his feet, head and bat in fluid unison. He could move forwards or back with no apparent effort and with no slowing of the bat's trajectory. He hit the ball hard, and almost always along the ground. Denis Compton said of him that he got into position 'quicker than any batsman I have ever seen'. Wilfred Rhodes said, 'No matter how you bowl to him, he seems to be able to place the ball just where he likes.'

Bradman was as vulnerable as any other player early in his innings. Jack Hobbs, for example, stood more chance, statistically, of reaching double figures, but once set Bradman was a freak. His chances of dismissal were a third less than anyone else's. Bradman played 80 Test innings. He passed fifty in 42 of them. In 29 of those he went on to pass a hundred. Twelve of those became double-centuries and two of those triple hundreds. In all Bradman passed a hundred in 36 per cent of his innings. Not only was his weight of scoring unprecedented, so was the rate. He still holds the records for the most hundreds scored in a single session of play (usually two hours), which he did six times, and the most runs scored in a day at 309.

With his strange grip and backlift, Bradman defied the coaching manual orthodoxy of the straight bat. The movements that he learned playing his childhood game turned him into cricket's most effective batsman and yet his method has never been adopted or taught by anyone. When Bradman himself was asked why, he replied, 'it's because they are coached not to do it. It's a different technique.' It has occurred naturally in some players, most notably in the great George Headley, who grew up playing baseball and was known as 'the Black Bradman'. Headley has a Test batting average of 60.83, the third highest of all time, and made ten centuries in his 40 innings. Rare film of W. G. Grace suggests that he also looped his bat towards gully, as do two of the modern game's heaviest scorers, Shivnarine Chanderpaul and Hashim Amla.

Perhaps Bradman was the most prodigious of all of the game's prodigies – in his childhood he reinvented the way the game should be played.

At Fleet Cricket Club we had a prodigy of our own. His name was Simon Massey. Simon's dad was in the first team, and had once hit Garry Sobers for four. Simon was only three or four years older than us but he'd already won a national newspaper competition to find a spin bowler and the rumour was that Hampshire were looking at him and might sign him up as a professional. The first time I saw him play was in an Under-17s game when he opened the batting and smashed the ball around with a certainty that I couldn't then define but somehow knew that I didn't have. Then he opened the bowling, not spin but quick stuff and he *was* quick. In the field he chased after everything and threw the ball miles. The action seemed to be pulled by gravity towards him, whatever he was doing. Both teams were drawn to him, too. At the end, they all seemed to want to shake his hand and hang around

with him. He immediately joined Barry Richards and
Geoffrey Boycott on my imaginary England team sheet.
Whenever I saw Simon playing or messing around in the
nets, he wore a floppy white sunhat, and I wanted one
badly. That summer there seemed to be no cooler sight
in all the world than I would cut walking out to bat in a
floppy white sunhat. My dad finally got hold of one, but
it was slightly too small and made of a strange kind of
stretch nylon. 'That looks like a hairnet,' Simon said when
he saw it. Everyone laughed but I wore it anyway and he
took it as the act of hero-worship that it was. Everything
about him seemed designed for cricket. He was good at
the game and, more than that, he was good at the stuff
that surrounded the game. He cracked the dressing-room
jokes, came up with nicknames, made the journeys to
away games fun – all of the things that I wasn't comfortable with and couldn't do, and that I was coming to realise
were as important as the actual playing. Simon was a natural cricketer and a natural athlete and I was far from both,
even with the totemic sunhat crushed onto my head. He
worked at it, too. He was into going to the gym in an age
when it was still known as 'weight-training'. The nearest place was in a leisure centre about five miles away
and once Simon could drive he started, at the request of
my dad, taking me over there with him, a weekly ritual
that I dreaded and loathed from the moment it was suggested. Simon would get under the bench press or the lat
machine and power out the reps and then I had to go over
and, humiliatingly, move the weights down to the lowest
amounts and try to shift them with my pipe-cleaner arms.
I spent most of the time trying to avoid doing anything at

all, wiping away non-existent sweat from my head with a towel and hovering by the water dispenser trying to look distracted.

The upside was that Simon inducted me into the group of players that were always at the ground. There were the Stone brothers, both tall and rake-thin purveyors of bouncy medium-pace; an immaculate opening bat called Martyn who possessed a Gray-Nicolls Scoop, the bat that everyone yearned for, and sometimes the club's opening bowler, a local PE teacher called Dinger Bell. Dinger had collar-length Jeff Thomson-style hair and a biblical beard and bowled from a thrillingly long run that made him much feared in the local leagues. In the nets he would come at us from a few paces, but it still felt like facing Thommo himself, especially in the club's lone outdoor lane, which was a concrete slab with a thin green mat pinned over it from which the ball skidded unpredictably. Simon usually bowled quickly, too, but it was in that net that I first faced his off-spin, which he began from a long, curved run that gave him the energy to create drift and bounce.

The event that would shape me more than any other single day of cricket came in one of those first, endless summers when it was announced that Hampshire were to play the Fleet CC first XI in a benefit match, and in a way that would make my real and imaginary worlds collide, the beneficiary was to be Barry Richards.* Not only would I see the great man playing cricket right in front

---

*I looked up Richards' benefit year while writing: it was 1977, which would have made me 12.

of me, he would be playing cricket on the same ground that I did, walking on the same grass, breathing the same air . . .

In my mind it lingers as a golden summer afternoon, the ground green and tree-lined and vivid in the heat. From nowhere, miraculously, a crowd had appeared to ring the boundary. I'd never seen the place where I played cricket look anything like it did that day. We'd been there for hours, anxious for the Hampshire team to arrive. When they did it was not, as I'd imagined, by luxury team coach, but in dribs and drabs in their cars, a couple of them sponsored and with their names painted on the sides, the rest just regular motors with cricketers and their gear crammed into them, like us but not like us. And then the moment came. Barry Richards drove down the laneway in a red sponsored car, parked it behind the pavilion and got out. From the boot he drew his shimmering Excalibur, a slender Gray-Nicolls with its deep red stripe down the spine. The next time I saw him, he was padded up, from which I gathered that Hampshire would be batting first regardless of who won the toss.

Barry Richards walked out onto the ground wearing his blue Hampshire cap, under it the same fuzz of hair and teeth that I'd seen on TV in the John Player League. Now he was here in front of me, in the flesh. I was almost levitating with joy. Barry took guard. Opening the bowling was Dinger Bell, coming in off his long run. Optimistically, he placed a couple of slips and a gully. Simon lurked in the covers in his white sunhat, on the same field as Barry Richards.

Dinger ran in. Barry Richards let the first ball go past his off-stump.

'Blimey,' I thought. 'Maybe even *Barry Richards* thinks Dinger Bell is quick . . .' Dinger ran in again. This one was shorter and on a good line. Richards adjusted his cap and fiddled with his thigh pad – well, he might have done: he certainly had enough time to. He moved easily to the leg-side as he waited for the ball to arrive and, then lifting the glowing Gray-Nicolls horizontally, he caressed the ball over the wicketkeeper's head. It was still going up when it crossed the freshly painted boundary line. Decades later, when Sachin Tendulkar popularised the ramp shot and everyone marvelled at it, I thought, 'I saw Barry Richards do that at Fleet Cricket Club . . .'

He made a dutiful and crowd-pleasing sixty-odd before retiring to the pavilion. I still recall one that he hit over the trees, out of the ground and on to the first hole of the pitch and putt course. And I still recall the only words that Barry Richards has, so far, ever spoken to me: 'Not now I'm having my sandwich', a sentence uttered gently while we hassled him for an autograph during tea.

When Simon went in to bat he was caught on the boundary by Richard Gilliat, the Hampshire captain. It was the sort of chance that a village cricketer would have dropped, from a meaty, low-flying pull shot that barely got above head height, but Gilliat pouched it so unfussily that he might have been catching an underarm lob. It was another of the early signs that I was seeing of just how big the game was, how much there was contained within it. Two seasons later, Simon was on the Hampshire staff, a professional cricketer, Barry Richards was no longer playing and Richard Gilliat was no longer captain and I was starting to understand that everything permanent was subject to change.

I think everyone who loves cricket has a moment like this; one that binds them to the game and brings it alive in a magical way. Mine was Barry Richards. Within a couple of seasons I'd left Fleet CC for a club just over the border in Surrey at Wrecclesham, where my dad had heard they had some good young players. They had: a combative pair of brothers, both all-rounders, called Ian and Alan Thorpe, and their tiny younger brother Graham, barely bigger than the bat but already a good left-hander; another pair of siblings, the Charters, Martin an elegant opener, Steve a nippy seamer; a genuinely quick bowler called Andy Partridge who had a slingy action a bit like Thommo's and who hit me twice in the same spot on an unprotected thigh in the nets once with consecutive deliveries (I still remember the pain, the second one felt like a knife going in); a wonderfully accurate seam bowler called Graham Larby, who once almost single-handedly bowled out Frensham for a team total of seven, and lots more. We played all over Surrey in various cups and knockouts, at Frensham's tiny bowl near the ponds, where an edge through the slips could sometimes go for six; at picture-perfect Tilford with its thatched pub, the Barley Mow, where you had to cross the road in front of the pavilion as you went in to bat; at Rowledge and The Bourne and Churt, and at Farnham, our local rivals who played on their hilltop ground by the side of the castle . . . many of them evening games, racing against the dipping sun to the finish, the time of day that I still find the most magical to play.

The Charter brothers also played for Basingstoke, a far bigger club with good connections to the Hampshire county side, so I started playing for them, too. Their home ground was May's Bounty, where John Arlott, a Basingstoke boy, had grown up watching from the leafy boundary, and which I saw for the first time one summer's evening for a trial in the nets, that were cut up at the top of field near the scoreboard and the old school wall. Hampshire played a couple of matches per year there, one county game and a John Player Sunday League match, and we were allowed to operate the scoreboard for them, any hint of slackness leading to an instantaneous and bad-tempered phone call from the Hampshire scorer Vic Isaacs. The dressing-rooms were at the top of the pavilion, which had its own balcony, and we'd sit up there trying to look like professionals. It was a buzz to score runs out on the Bounty, where I'd watched Boycott play a Sunday League match, once carried Jeff Thomson's bag up the pavilion stairs when he had a season with Middlesex, and saw the West Indies star Alvin Kallicharran, a tiny man, smash ball after ball down the ground, over the hedge and into the road beyond.

Simon qualified as a coach and got a winter job at Alf's. After my lessons with Jim Cameron, I'd stay on and bowl a few overs for him when his arm got tired towards the end of the day, and then Simon would drive us back home down the A3 at high speed in his junk-filled car, him telling funny, mostly unprintable stories about the other players at Hampshire. Every Saturday for longer than anyone could remember, a guy called Joe would come in for a net. It was usually booked for the last half-hour, and I'd often bowl to him while Jim lounged at the back of the lane telling Joe exactly the same things he'd told him a thousand times before. Joe didn't mind. He'd have been drinking brown ale in the bar since lunchtime, so he wasn't that bothered about what the bowling was like or what Jim had to say about his batting. I used to wonder what Joe was doing at Gover's, why he came or what he got out of it. It wasn't until some years later that I realised he was alone and just needed somewhere to go. Gover's was his place.

Simon somehow discovered when Joe's birthday was, and organised a whip-round. We got him a little trophy of a batsman and had it inscribed, and a silver tankard for his brown ale. After his net, all of the coaches, Alf's son John who ran the shop downstairs, Terry the barman and even Alf, fresh from the office, crept into the snooker room and gave them to him. It was the first time I'd ever seen a man cry.

3

The Fabric

When I feel like a little cricketing psychogeography, I don't have to travel far. Within a few miles of where I was born, first played and live now came three men who would help to pull the game from its scattered origins into a recognisable form. The lives of David Harris, 'Silver Billy' Beldham and Frederick Beauclerk, who grew up and lived on the north-east borders of Hampshire and Surrey, contained within them cricket archetypes that have recurred throughout time: the feared fast bowler; the charismatic batsman; the autocratic, entitled captain and administrator. Did they create them, or were they always there, inherent and integral, somehow built into the warp and weft of cricket's design?

Three miles from home is Hartley Wintney, where the village green, flanked on one side by a pub, on another by some towering oaks and a third by picture-book tumble-down cottages, has been standing since 1770, making it perhaps the oldest continuously played on cricket ground in England. Like many very old grounds, it slopes from one side to the other and is full of swales and hollows that shimmer magically in summer light. Even in winter, when dogs gallop across the frosty outfield, it's possible to stand there and feel the game deep in the earth.

David Harris was born a mile or so away in Elvetham in 1755 and learned his cricket on the green, known then as Hartley Row. He came into a game in which batsmen defended two stumps, the height and the width of them recently standardised: they stood 22in tall and 6in apart, with a bail on top. Soon afterwards the middle stump was added when Lumpy Stevens bowled John Small three times during a game at the Artillery Ground, the ball passing through the wicket without disturbing the bail. These changes made Harris into something not seen before: a length bowler, a man who learned to use the condition of the pitch to discomfort the batsman.

Facing David Harris must have been an extraordinary thing. He was difficult to hit and dangerous to confront, the proto-tearaway, an unforgiving man for an unforgiving game. The experience was described by John Nyren of Hambledon in his memoir, *The Cricketers of My Time*. 'He was the very best bowler,' Nyren wrote, 'a bowler who, between anyone and himself, comparison must fail.' Harris would raise the ball to the height of his forehead 'like a soldier at drill' before stepping forwards as his arm swirled towards the batsman 'with a twist', the ball appearing to be 'pushed out' as it flew from his hand. From Nyren's account Harris sounds almost like a side-arm bowler: he generated lift as well as pace, and many a player had his knuckles ground against the bat handle which, in a time before gloves, would have produced plenty of pain and blood.

It was a new phenomenon but one that would snake its way through the next two centuries: a fast bowler could induce fear in the opposition, producing mental anguish to accompany the possibility of physical harm. The playwright Frederick Reynolds, a keen amateur, wrote of facing Harris: 'I felt almost as if taking my ground in a duel . . . and my terrors were so much increased by the mock pity and sympathy of Hammond, Beldham, and others round the wicket, that when this mighty bowler, this *Jupiter Tonans*, hurled his bolt at me, I shut my eyes in the intensity of my panic, and mechanically gave a random desperate blow.'

Much of the psychological dimension of the modern game is present in the emotions of the batsman – the loneliness and the fear are lurking, just waiting to come out. The fielders Hammond and Beldham compound it with sarcasm: sledging existed then, too.

David Harris must have lived a gentle, rural life away from the violence of the crease. The family moved from Elvetham to Crookham, a few miles east, and he would have walked across the fields and the heathland between to reach Hartley Row. He worked as a potter, never married and during the long winters he practised his bowling in a barn. All the while his reputation began to grow, perhaps the first knuckle-busting, dread-inducing paceman in history.

Five miles in the other direction is Farnham's hilltop ground. Farnham's first game was played on 13 August 1782 at their early home at Holt Pound, a patch of scrub still visible behind the local pub. It was known as 'the Oval', from where the ground at Kennington would later take its name. That first match, against Odiham, marked the debut of the 16-year-old William 'Silver Billy' Beldham, who would become the greatest batsman of the under-arm age (as well as a sledger of Frederick Reynolds). Billy was born on a farm near Wrecclesham in February 1766, the start of an epically long and significant life. Along with David Harris, Beldham was to be an agent of change in a changing game. They first faced one another in 1784 when Farnham played Hambledon – Silver Billy wrote in his *Reminiscences* of 1836 that he made 43 and was watched by the Earl of Winchilsea, who became his patron.

It's impossible to know how many runs Silver Billy scored or how many wickets David Harris took because records of the age are irregular and incomplete. Wickets were only put down to a bowler when the batsman was actually bowled – catches were given to the fielder. Billy's 'known' career credits him with 7,045 runs in 189 matches, with a best of 144. Harris took 328 wickets in 78 games. Their significance is not in the numbers but best measured in the technical advances that they made, in the teams that they turned out for and the legends that they left.

The history of cricket can be seen as a giant game of call and response between bat and ball, the evolution of one shaping change in the other. David Harris began bowling his spearing, kicking length and forced a reply from bats-men used to standing back in their crease and swinging hard across the line with the distinctive curved bats of the age. A new shape of bat was required to quell the threat. In the fields of Farnham, Silver Billy and his elder brother George were schooled by Harry Hall in presenting this new-style straight bat vertically to the ball by keeping the left elbow high. Billy became, in the words of John Nyren, 'safer than the bank'. As his star rose Beldham began moving out towards the ball to drive, punishing the too full delivery and helping to nullify erratic bounce. Harry Walker, born a few miles up the road from Billy in Churt, unveiled the cut shot to the ball pitched short. Suddenly the new bowling had new batting to contend with.

Silver Billy introduced another notion to batting too. Tall for his time at 5ft 9, and something of a dandy – the 'Silver Billy' nickname came from his flowing blond locks – he made batting *beautiful*. He turned the batsman into the focus of attention, heroically alone in a team game. 'He was one of the most beautiful sights that can be imagined, and which would have delighted an artist, was to see him make himself up to hit a ball,' John Nyren wrote. 'It was the beau ideal of grace, animation, and concentrated energy.' As Billy is said to have fathered 39 children, it's safe to say that his aesthetic appeal extended far beyond the crease.

After Billy's first encounter with David Harris, they would cross swords often. Thirty miles to the west, a field by a public house near Hambledon would become the centre of the game, and each journeyed there many times. It's from these experiences that we learn most about them, tantalising fractions of a story that existed in a context that is lost to us forever.

The Bat and Ball pub stands two miles outside Hambledon, and looks out over Broadhalfpenny Down. The ground itself lies on a ridge that connects to Salt Hill, a famous slope down which the fielders, in the days before boundaries, would have to charge. The proximity of pub and ground are important: the landlord of the Bat and Ball was Richard Nyren, who was a formidable all-round cricketer, the first well-known left-handed bat and the on-field 'general' of Hambledon and Hampshire (the two being, at first, interchangeable).

He was also responsible for feeding and watering the players and must have been pretty decent at that if his own generous dimensions are anything to go by – 5ft 9in and 'very stout' yet 'uncommonly active'.

The Down was common land on which horse racing and hare coursing were popular and the cricket soon drew raucous crowds, many of them wanting to bet on the action. An early game between Hambledon and Dartford is recorded because the Reverend Keats of Chaldon lost his dog in the throng and placed an advertisement for its return in the *Reading Chronicle*. Another, between Hambledon and Coulsden, was recorded by John Baker in his diary, and describes a two-day journey by horseback from Chichester in order to attend.

Yet the words that place the club at the centre of cricket's early history come from Richard Nyren's son John. He was born in 1764, the year his father first played for Hambledon, his childhood suffused in cricket and cricketers. Although he could play, John, like many sons of great fathers that would follow, played in shadow. He may have been a footnote, known only for his appearances in the inaugural Gentlemen versus Players matches, had he not written about the game. And John Nyren the author is almost all we have of the era. He even described his father with a gimlet, albeit affectionate, eye: 'I never saw a finer specimen of the thoroughbred old English yeoman.'

John Nyren worked with Charles Cowden Clarke, poet, teacher, Shakespearian scholar and perhaps the first pre-eminent sporting ghost writer, on Nyren's *The Cricketers of My Time*, which first appeared as a serial in *The Town* magazine, before being redrafted and used as the second part of *The Young Cricketer's Tutor*. Through Cowden Clarke's shaping of Nyren's memories, we have something tantalising and distant, rich enough in cricketing detail for John Arlott to call it 'still the finest study of cricket and cricketers ever written', but which stands outside of the society that it came from.

'His narrative is rich in character studies of the players but silent upon their lives and views,' wrote John Major in *More Than a Game*, his study of cricket's origins. 'What did this mixture of honest yeomen and simple rustics think of the society in which they lived? How did they react when they left Broadhalfpenny Down to play matches in the sprawl of London? Did they know anything of the political turmoil of the wars against France, of the American Revolution and the fall of Lord North's government? What opinions did they have of twenty-four-year-old William Pitt the Younger becoming Prime Minister? Did they know Captain James Cook had discovered Australia? Nyren is silent on all these issues.'

An explanation may be that cricket – and sport – didn't yet demand contextualising. It hadn't occupied the place in the consciousness that it now does. It was simply something to do, and here were the men good at doing it: stout Dick Nyren; the great batsman John Small (Nyren may have been the first to coin the expression 'star' to describe a sportsman when he said Small 'had the lustre of a star');

Lamborn, a bowler not granted the dignity of a first name in the text, but the first recorded purveyor of spin, then so new that Nyren called it 'twist'; Lumpy Stevens, whose accuracy brought the introduction of a middle stump; and, of course, David Harris and Silver Billy Beldham.

Nyren's book was published 40 years after the players he describes had stopped playing, so his memory is lamplit and nostalgic, the era already gone. Hambledon's spell as cricket's foremost club was brief: the Marylebone Cricket Club moved to Lord's in 1787, and the sport began to shed its rural roots and take its place in metropolitan society.

Silver Billy lived to see it happen. He played on until he was 55 years old, making the 30-mile journey from Farnham to Hambledon by horse. As his fame spread, he was contracted to play in matches across the south, earning more than twice the annual salary of a labourer from playing cricket. When he was done, he retired to run the Barley Mow at Tilford. He made cricket bats in the back room, and retained his remarkable vigour deep into old age. He walked the seven hilly miles that separate Tilford from Farnham at the age of 84 just to watch a game. The summer before he died at the age of 96 he was received with all honours at Lord's and had his name advertised at The Oval to help draw a crowd to a match billed as 'Old Versus Young'. 'Old Beldham died last winter,' reported *London Society* in 1862 – and all knew who they meant.

David Harris was not so lucky. He was beset by gout, which ended his career in 1798. He went out with a bang, taking five wickets for All England against Surrey at Lord's (on Thomas Lord's first ground at Dorset Square rather than the current site) before retreating to his solitary potter's life in Crookham, where he died five years later. He was 48, exactly half the time on earth granted Silver Billy.

It was a rogue's game at first. It took the Victorians to make cricket synonymous with fair play, 'second only to Christianity' as John Major put it. In the years of Silver Billy it was a gamblers' day out, the players contracted as 'given men' to teams with patrons willing to pay them. Conflicts of interest were barely considered. Lord Frederick Beauclerk, a descendant of Charles II and his mistress Nell Gwynn, lived for most of his life in Winchfield, two or three miles from Elvetham and the home of David Harris. Joining cricket's archetypal quickie and show-pony batsman came the third of the triumvirate, a man who yearned not only to play the game but to control it too. Beauclerk was both a vicar and a doctor of divinity, although his sermons, when he could be bothered to give them, were famously dull and the clerical life merely cover for a cricketing career. Beauclerk had a volcanic temper on the field and a vindictive nature off it, and in a sport already given to romanticising its stars, 'an unqualified eulogy was never seen'. He claimed to make more than £600 per season from betting on matches – a phenomenal sum for the time.

Playing in a big-money single-wicket contest with Thomas Howard against the crack pair of George Osbaldeston and William Lambert, he refused to postpone the match when Osbaldeston was taken ill during the first innings – 'play or pay,' he is reputed to have said. Lambert responded by continually bowling wide, and Beauclerk became so angry he and Howard lost the game – and Beauclerk's money – by 15 runs. The feud ran for years. First Beauclerk had wide bowling outlawed by the Marylebone Cricket Club. Then, after an ill-tempered match between his All England team and a Nottingham side that had Osbaldeston and Lambert in it gave rise to accusations of fixing, Beauclerk had Lambert banned from ever playing at Lord's. When Osbaldeston later resigned from MCC after another contentious single-wicket match, Beauclerk refused to readmit him.

Beauclerk lived by his own code. He lobbied MCC to have round-arm bowling outlawed but claimed many wagers won for him by the round-arm bowler John Willes. He took his 'nasty' dog to Lord's every time he went despite the animal being banned, and campaigned hard against the use of leg-guards until Alfred Mynn almost had to have his leg amputated after being struck repeatedly during a match in which Beauclerk was his non-playing captain. The cricket historian Rowland Bowen called him 'a cleric without, it would seem, the faintest interest in being a clergyman or any kind of Christian'. More precisely, he was 'foul-mouthed, dishonest . . . he bought and sold matches as though they were lots at an auction'.

In this, though, Beauclerk was not alone. In his *Reminiscences*, Silver Billy recalled: 'You may hear that I sold matches. I will confess I once was sold myself by two men, one of whom would not bowl, and the other would not bat his best, and lost ten pounds. The next match, at Nottingham, I joined in selling, and got my money back. But for this once, I could say I never was bought in my life; and this was not for want of offers from C and other turfmen, though often I must have been accused. For where it was worth while to buy, no man could keep a character; because to be out without runs or to miss a catch was, by the disappointed betting-men, deemed proof as strong as Holy Writ.'

Billy was no angel, despite his celestial hair. He loaded one side of the ball with mud during a game between a Three (a three-man team) of Surrey (Billy, alongside Lambert and Robinson) against – perhaps unsurprisingly – a Three of England led by Beauclerk. The ball took 'an extraordinary twist' and bowled Beauclerk, and Billy was heard boasting about his subterfuge in the pub after the game.

Beauclerk's unpopularity was lifelong and hard-earned. He fancied himself as a dandy at the wicket, wearing a white beaver-skin hat and fine breeches with a scarlet sash, and would sometimes dangle a gold watch from his middle stump to imply that his defence was impregnable. He could certainly play – he could bat, bowl and was one of the first to appreciate the importance of good fielding – and he studied his opponents' game for weaknesses. He had physical courage. He played on with a badly broken finger sustained in the match which he'd successfully accused Lambert of fixing and suffered an infection that nearly cost him his life. He was also obsessed by the game: one of the most generous descriptions of him came from a famous courtesan called Harriette Wilson, who called him 'a sly, shy, odd man, not very communicative unless one talks of cricket'. He ascended to the presidency of MCC, a position from which he unilaterally did everything from select teams to alter the Laws of the game.

Perhaps the writer who has thrown the gentlest light on him is John Major, who knows the weight of public scorn himself. 'Lord's still drew Beauclerk as an old man to all the great games,' he wrote, 'and he sat there, his white dog at his feet, observing all in solitary reflection of a life devoted to cricket and, in character to the last, totally indifferent to the verdict of history.' Yet a life as unyielding as his left little in the way of goodwill. On his death at 76 in the chill April of 1850, *The Times* refused to print an obituary.

There are echoes of the angst that David Harris created ('I felt almost as if taking my ground in a duel') in Bob Woolmer's description of being struck on the pad by Michael Holding ('the pain was so incredible I thought I'd been shot'). Beldham's raffish, silky run-making began a lineage that runs through C. B. Fry, Victor Trumper, Peter May, Neil Harvey, David Gower, V. V. S. Laxman and A. B. de Villiers. And Beauclerk's haughty worldview, with its early hints of empire-building, has characterised almost every phase of cricket administration. Other parts of the game, the hardships of travel, the acceptance of pain and physical labour, gambling, match-fixing, gamesmanship, rivalry, sharp practice . . . they were in the earliest seeding of its universe.

And then came cricket's first colossus, the prototype fast-bowling, big-hitting, crowd-pleasing all-rounder, a man who did not just make a difficult game look easy, he made it look brutal and brilliant and new. They nicknamed Alfred Mynn 'the Lion of Kent', and like the giant all-rounders that would follow him – Keith Miller, Imran Khan, Ian Botham, Andrew Flintoff – there was something about him that chimed with the public. They loved him unconditionally. Perhaps his size had something to do with that: he stood well over 6ft and was almost as wide, bull-chested and broad. He weighed 21 stone, a big fellow now but in the era in which he lived a giant. And perhaps it was his nature, religious and humble and brave. Certainly it was his cricket and in particular his bowling. Mynn took six steps up to the wicket and then whipped that giant right arm around his body and hurled the ball into the uneven turf. Over the course of a decade more than a thousand men fell to his bowling – and those are just the first-class wickets. Mynn would become the unbeatable king of a type of game that was not new but that would have its brief years in the sun. Just as Twenty20 cricket blazed into the pro game almost two hundred years later, the single wicket format was about to have its zeitgeist moment, filled with star players and built for gambling, a type of cricket that would burn quickly and brightly and enrapture the public as it did so.

First Mynn had to recover from that heroic and disastrous innings in 1836 at Leicester when Beauclerk was his non-playing captain, and, *sans* leg-guards, he was struck repeatedly by Sam Redgate. He was despatched to London on the stage coach immediately after play. Once he arrived, the attending surgeon, Dr Lawrence, informed him that his leg was so badly damaged that it would be amputated at the hip. Mynn asked for a few minutes to say his prayers: surgery in 1836 was carried out without anaesthetic and was both terrifying and deadly. As Mynn prayed, Lawrence changed his mind and, although it took two years, Mynn eventually regained full use of the limb.

Single-wicket was a way of pitting small teams of men against one another. A game could be made between two players, or teams of two or three. Rules were informal, with the participants able to negotiate the terms of the contest. A game between two players generally involved each man having a nominated number of fielders. A 'bounds' was marked, usually horizontal with the batting crease, and no hit ending up behind it could be scored from (bounds were sometimes abandoned in matches with four or more fielders). Its other distinguishing feature was that the batsman was required to run to the bowler's end and back to register a single. Both competitors could be exhausted by the effort. In 1827 a farmer called Francis Trumper used his sheepdog to defeat a Two of Middlesex, the dog standing by his master as he ran up to the wicket before retrieving the ball 'with such a wonderful quickness it was difficult to get a run even from a long hit'. It was a trick repeated by the innkeeper Silas Quartermain of Streatham Common, who trained his terrier to field for him. The writer E. V. Lucas told the apocryphal story of a single-wicket contest between two 80-year-olds. The first batted and made 12, and then watched in astonishment as his opponent staggered exhausted to the pavilion leaving his wicket to be bowled down. The batsman, also exhausted, bowled 13 wides in succession and lost.

Single-wicket was also a mano-a-mano challenge, and Alfred Mynn was the most imposing of opponents. He was physically dominant and earned his mighty nickname the Lion of Kent after the first of his victories over Tom

Hills, the champion of the county. Facing Mynn presented almost every challenge. His bowling, always around the wicket, was rapid and parsimonious, and in single-wicket play even harder to attack because behind-the-stumps deflections went into the bounds and could not be scored from. His own batting, by contrast, was built on powerful straight hitting.

Then there were the intangibles. The crowds loved Mynn, and he loved a crowd — away from cricket his hobby was amateur dramatics. He also needed the money. He was made bankrupt in 1845 and served a brief time in prison as a debtor. Some said he was still trying to pay medical bills incurred during his two years out injured.

The acknowledged champion of single-wicket was Mynn's Kent team-mate and close friend Fuller Pilch, the most elegant batsman in the land. Such was the clamour for them to meet, a letter, purported to be from Mynn challenging Pilch, was printed by *Bell's Life* magazine. It turned out to be a fake written by a desperate fan.

Pilch declined the contest with his friend and instead Mynn defeated James Dearman for the title Champion of England and a prize of £100. Mynn was utterly dominant, winning the first match by 123 runs to 11 and the second by an innings and 36 in front of huge crowds.

He went unchallenged for another eight years until the most famous single-wicket match of them all. His opponent was Nicholas Felix, another of Kent's legendary five ('And with five such cricketers it was natural to win/As Felix, Wenman, Hillyer, Fuller Pilch and Alfred Mynn' ran a celebratory verse). 'Felix' was actually a pseudonym. His given name was Nicholas Wanostrocht, but, having inherited a school from his father, he felt that cricket might be seen as too frivolous a pursuit for a headmaster who was just 27 years old and perhaps lacking the gravitas to tease fees from the selective rich. His fame as a player meant that his identity soon became common knowledge, but Felix it was, and what a man he became: musician, painter, writer, scholar, inventor and sportsman. Fuller Pilch was particularly enamoured of his ability to produce a tune from almost any instrument. His mind was restlessly creative. He invented the first bowling machine, which he christened 'the Catapulta', and the first batting gloves, which he made by sticking strips of India rubber along the fingers. He batted with rubber padding under his long socks too. His watercolours of other cricketers were widely admired, and as a writer he produced an early classic of the game, the rather beautifully titled *Felix on the Bat*, published in 1845. It had a subtitle too, 'Being A Scientific Inquiry Into The Use Of The Cricket Bat', and was one of the first pieces of writing to explore technique, or in Felix's own vivid phrase 'how to wield this mighty sceptre of delight'. He was already conscious of batting's psychological dimension: 'Defend until the excitement of your important position in the game shall subside.' And like Bob Woolmer and Tim Noakes centuries later, he was in thrall to the unlikeliness of it all too: 'Astounding is not a term half powerful enough to describe the electrical rapidity with which the eye communicates to the nerves, and the nerves to the muscles the word of command.'

The batting of Nicholas Felix was as quick and as nimble as his mind. He believed that the man on strike should be crouched and ready – 'observe the first position in fencing – en garde!' A left-hander noted for the brilliance of his offside play, especially a rapier-like cut shot, Fuller Pilch rated him as the most attractive batsman in England, although not the safest. Stonewalling was not in his nature. When pitted against Alfred Mynn, in single-wicket, his other disadvantage was his bowling, underarm slow lobs.

The contest was set for 18 June 1846 at Lord's, with two hundred guineas to the winner. Mynn, two years younger, almost a foot taller and twice the size of his opponent, was the betting favourite. Each man was given two fielders. The first innings were over quickly, Felix splintering his bat try- ing to get off the mark and being bowled next ball, and then Mynn caught and bowled for five – a rifle-crack of a straight drive that Felix held more in self-preservation than intent ('I only had time to put up my hand to save my life').

Then came one of the most remarkable passages of cricket ever played, the thronging crowd caught up in the drama of a duel in which Mynn bowled 247 deliveries to Felix, who, with considerable skill, struck 175 of them. His frustration must have been huge as the vast majority of his hits fell in the bounds behind the wicket. In all he scored just three runs, plus one wide bowled by the apparently indefatigable giant who faced him. It was a battle of Felix's will and Mynn's power. Finally, as Felix must have felt his opponent was on the verge of weakening, Mynn got one through his defences to win by an innings and one run. The match had taken almost five hours, in which nine runs were scored.

The drama was such that a rematch was arranged immediately, set for 29 and 30 September in Bromley on open ground by the White Hart pub. The two stars of

Kent once more drew large crowds. The gentry gathered in marquees erected especially for the match. Mynn won again, passing Felix's total of 12 in his second innings.

Even as he did so, the brief boom time of single wicket was ending. The expansion of the railways made it far easier to transport entire teams around the country and Mynn and Felix were enthusiastic members of one of the first, William Clarke's All England XI.

The public appetite for spectacle and weirdness remained strong. The sport was about to yield to Victorian rectitude but not quite yet. In the same summer that single-wicket died out, 2,400 people gathered at the Priory Grounds in Lewisham to watch a team of one-armed men play a team of one-legged men, a lurid, almost macabre fixture that had been played twice before, in 1796 and 1841 (although, as a vivid report in *The Australian* newspaper noted: 'during this long recess, the great leveller had bowled a large proportion of those who figured on that occasion out.')

The players from both teams were Greenwich Pensioners, navy men who had been injured in service during the Napoleonic Wars and now lived at the Royal Hospital. What a sight it was. *The Australian* was clear on the nature of the spectacle and the motivation of the crowd: 'Novelty was the ruling passion. Nine tenths went merely for the say of the thing . . . The singularity of the Greenwich dress combined with the ludicrous positions of the fielders, their antique physiognomies and the general clumsiness of both parties at the game produced a match that was grotesque in the extreme.'

A clue as to what was in it for the players came from the description of their 'substantial luncheon before each day's play' and 'for their dinner there was a profusion of roast and boiled beef, and lamb, accompanied by plenty of heavy'.

In their veterans' uniforms, full of grub and with a night's worth of ale in them, before the baying, betting crowd ('the money in favour of the men with two living legs') the One-Arm XI made 50 in their first innings, which featured a top score of eight not out. The One-Legged XI replied with 32. The One-Arm XI extended their lead with 41, leaving the One-Legged XI 60 to win. They were dismissed for 44, a gallant effort that included the highest score of the match, 15, from their number five, Sears. The greatest contributor to both totals was extras – the One-Legged XI conceded 30, the One-Arm XI 43, all of which were wides. Across the match, 21 players were dismissed without scoring, and the One-Legged XI featured five batsmen who made pairs, including the unfortunate number 11 Baldrick, who was run out twice.

Then, in strange triumph, both teams 'marched to the Bull Inn, headed by an excellent band who had been engaged throughout the match. Each man had free passage to and from the Royal Hospital, a glass of grog to drink to Her Majesty's health and ten shillings for his two days' exertions.'

These are the names of the men who played that match:

One-Arm XI: Guay, Wiley, Morley, Johnson, Burns, Sissoms, Broom, Newsom, Seale, Jeffreys, Sowden.

One-Legged XI: Wetherhead, Ryan, Scot, Brown, Sears, Albar, Polston, West, Drew, Browne, Baldrick.

★

The summer of 1848 saw the birth of William Gilbert Grace. It is a distant place, 1848. Brahms was 15. Tolstoy was 20. Dickens had just written *A Christmas Carol*. The Crimean War was five years in the future. America had 30 states. It was the Year of Revolutions in France, Austria, Denmark, Hungary, Poland, Italy and the Netherlands. Not much of this touched the village of Downend, near Bristol, where Grace grew up in a house called The Chestnuts with its sun-dappled orchard where he first played cricket. The man who would become the great emblem of the Victorian era lived in an uncanny echo of the monarch herself – both Victoria and Albert and WG's parents, Henry and Martha, had nine children. As he and his siblings learned the game under the eye of the formidable Martha (who would allow her girls only to field) and her brother Alfred Pocock, so the men and the game that Grace would consign to history began to pass. Felix was struck by a mysterious paralysis and retired from cricket in 1854. Mynn died suddenly at his brother Walter's house in 1861. He saw only the start of the decade in which cricket once more felt the shock of the new. As Grace debuted in 1864, a 15-year-old prodigy, overarm bowling was legalised.

Over the next four decades, Grace became the alpha and omega of the game. You can look into him and see whatever aspect you want, because it is there. He was its great leap forward into modernity. He, and the men who ultimately succeeded him as cricket's most famous players, the regal Ranjitsinhji, inventor of the leg glance, and C. B. Fry, the polymath 'Golden God' of the early twentieth century, knitted the game into the wider social fabric of the age, where it took on a resonance and meaning that still exist.

Some forces arrive from nowhere and what they do and what they know are to a degree unexplainable. Shakespeare produced 39 plays, finished *The Tempest* and then barely wrote another word. Where did he come from? James Joyce was beaten up one night on St Stephen's Green, Dublin, was helped home by an elderly man called Alfred H. Hunter and from that came *Ulysses*. How did Einstein understand the universe through maths? Why did Bobby Fischer know all of chess and almost nothing of anything else? These are human mysteries of various scales, and Grace was one of them. In the summer of 1860, when he was 11 years old, he made a score of 51 for West Gloucestershire against Clifton, a total of which Beldham or Felix would have been proud in adulthood. By the time he was 18, Grace was acknowledged as the finest player in England. That summer, he made his maiden first-class century, 224 not out, at The Oval and 'was thenceforward the biggest name in cricket'. In his first transcendent season, 1871, he accounted for ten of the 17 first-class hundreds scored in England and was declared 'the Champion' by *Lilywhites* magazine, a nickname that he kept until the end. He'd already grown the giant beard that created a brand a century before anyone knew what a brand was. He was the first man to score a hundred before lunch, the first to score a thousand runs and take a hundred wickets in the same season, the first to score a triple hundred. That came in 1876 against Kent at Canterbury – 344 not out. Two days later he made 177 against Nottinghamshire and two days after that 318 not out against Yorkshire, in all 839 runs in six days for once out. When he made his fiftieth first-class century, he had as many as the next 13 batsmen on the list added together.

Deep into his dotage, Fuller Pilch was taken to see Grace bat. He watched for a while and said, 'this man scores continuously from balls that old Fuller would have been thankful to stop'.

Pilch had identified the philosophical shift that Grace had brought to batting. With it, he had defined what the new intention of batsmanship was: not simply to stay in but to score runs. 'There was a prevailing idea at the time that as long as a bowler was straight the batsman could do nothing against him . . . that idea I determined to test,' Grace wrote. He developed a high lofted drive for the full ball and similarly airborne cut and pull shorts for the ball pitched short, each struck as hard as he could. That maiden 224 not out at The Oval was its first iteration. Bernard Darwin, grandson of Charles and a noted sports reporter, witnessed the game and wrote that Grace 'went on piling them up with a cheerful ruthlessness'.

The restless energy he threw into it crackled through the young Grace: it was also the innings that he interrupted overnight to rush from The Oval to Crystal Palace where, resplendent in his pink running knickerbockers and in front of a crowd of 10,000, he won the 440m hurdles (the recorder listing him soberly as 'Mr W. Grace'). Four weeks later he returned to The Oval and played perhaps an even better innings, 173 for the Gentlemen of the South against the Players, the ferocity of his hitting putting paid to his trusty bat in the process.

From then on Grace's method was built around attacking, even on pitches that wouldn't pass for the car park at glistening modern stadia. Lord's in particular was notorious – Grace would pick stones from the wicket as he batted and once jerked the crowd to its feet as he blocked out three consecutive 'shooters', wicked deliveries that didn't bounce at all but instead pitched and then flew along the ground.

Darwin again: 'He was no longer climbing the ladder, he had got to the top, although he was destined to add a few more rungs to it, dizzy rungs utterly beyond anyone else's reach.' Somehow he had looked at cricket and interpreted it in a way that turned it into something else, something that we could immediately recognise as the modern game. In doing so, he continued the great sequence of call and response between bat and ball that has travelled through the history of the game. First one dominates, as the ball did through cricket's beginnings, then the bat took hold.*

The maelstrom of change coalesced around him. Equipment standardised: pads and gloves became universal, bats were spliced. Overarm bowling fully replaced roundarm. The public turned away from single-wicket contests and the brief, bright flare of popularity for professional touring sides playing games against teams of local cricketers often twice their number – William Clarke became one of the first men to grow rich through cricket with

---

*At the moment, we are in another time of the bat; a response to the eras of Lillee and Thomson, West Indies' pace assault, the rise of reverse swing and the game's two most prolific spinners, Muttiah Muralitharan and Shane Warne.

his All England XI that featured Mynn, Felix and a young John Wisden and which specialised in these 'against-the-odds' matches — in favour of county cricket. Here was the game and here was its star, its conceptual force, arriving together and in perfect alignment. Through Victoria's empire, cricket spread — the outposts of empire remain its strongholds. The first victories of Australia, India and West Indies over the 'mother country' of England became significant moments of national identity. Their own greatest players — Don Bradman, Sunil Gavaskar, the Three Ws and more — made their legends by beating England. As latterly as 1996, Sri Lanka's World Cup win was another such lightning rod. Many of the game's impenetrable, internecine governance issues, the power struggle that has seen India become the new centre of world cricket and its de facto leader, have their roots in empire. In the bodyline series, and in Tests between India and Pakistan that led to political schisms; in the West Indies' 'blackwash' of England in 1984 that brought valediction to the Windrush generation; or the boycott of South Africa, the game's following has given it a unique reach. The story may be apocryphal, but Nelson Mandela's first question on leaving Robben Island was said to be 'is Bradman still alive?'.

All of this stands on Grace's giant shoulders, and the game has changed less in the years since his passing in 1915 than it did during his career, although he would find the world around it unrecognisable. Imagine explaining to him the concept of the internet or the Mars Rover. But sit him down at Adelaide Oval for the first day-night Test match that was played in 2015, and once he had got over the lights and the crowds and the stands, he would find a deep and comforting familiarity in the game that was being played, its shape and its duration. Grace, like the game he created, is still here, and he is still one of the most recognisable cricketers on earth. His fame, and the power of his impact, remain: when Monty Python wanted an image for the face of God in *The Life of Brian*, they chose Grace.

WG's love was lifelong, like Silver Billy's. There's something moving about the thought of old Billy setting out to walk from Tilford to Farnham to watch the cricket, as there is of Grace, the grand old man, retiring to Eltham and becoming the mustard-keen captain of their second XI at the age of 66. The game bore their shape, but their love for it was simple and enduring.

4
The Day of the Pig

I wanted to be a professional cricketer, and for a while I thought I might become one. The empirical evidence was sketchy at best, but I hadn't yet been stopped. I lived in the hazy dream world of a kid not awakened to the realities of the game and I seemed to be doing just enough to sustain the fantasy. I'd made a thousand runs in a season. I played in winning teams at good clubs. I'd been in a few district and representative sides and had played with or against most of the people in the county who seemed to be thought of as promising cricketers. More importantly perhaps, I'd had flashes of truth, little moments of revelation about what the game could be. Facing a quick left-arm opening bowler who'd played for a Wales Schools side, I leaned forward on a ball just outside off stump and barely felt it connect with the bat. It flew past cover to the boundary, one of the few times in my life I've timed the ball utterly perfectly. I hit the first five deliveries of a match against the Hampshire Hoggets for four and then got out trying to do the same to the sixth – I felt then like I usually only felt batting in the nets, free from pressure and the fear of failure, just smashing the ball for the fun of it. And I'd finally made a hundred, too – just. I'd got there pushing a single on the leg side. Back then the tradition was that a hundred was enough and the batsman should give up his wicket, so I took a big swing at the next ball. But I was seeing it well and it cleared the man they had put at long-on. I made sure I missed the next one and walked off. When I looked in the scorebook I'd got 105 – the scorer had miscounted and the single I'd pushed had only got me to 99.

But these moments seemed rare. In my heart I knew that the game filled me with fear. I secretly dreaded every step up, because before I took it I could live in the fantasy of not knowing. I was pretty sure that Barry Richards didn't feel that way. Cricket had become full of deep ambiguities – it was an unforgiving place, unaccepting of failure or weakness and yet those things were quotidian while playing it. I yearned for the kind of desire that Simon Massey and other guys I played with had, the kind that overwhelmed the fear and allowed them to relish the challenge.

Simon was established in Hampshire's second XI and had been twelfth man for the County Championship side on a few occasions. He'd even got Monte Lynch out when Hampshire seconds played Surrey seconds at Guildford. I could imagine how much Monte loved that. Simon called one day to say that Peter Sainsbury, the Hampshire coach, was having nets for some younger players so that he could cast his eye over them. Simon, to my consternation and my dad's delight, had got me in. I prayed for rain, but the morning dawned bright and hot. My dad took the day off work and we drove to Southampton, to the old Northlands Road ground, where I'd watched Barry Richards on television so many times. We got changed in the first-team dressing-room, which seemed just as ratty and damp as all of the other dressing-rooms I ever went in, the dark wood floor full of splinters brought up by the players' spikes.

'Barry Richards changed here,' I thought. Changed here, propped his bats against the wall, sat on the benches once he was out . . .

The nets were behind one of the stands, by the car park. There were five or six of us there. I recognised a couple of the other lads. Peter Sainsbury came out and told us that we'd all get a bat and a bowl and then we'd have some lunch and have another net in the afternoon, so there was plenty of time to relax and enjoy it. In the morning I batted okay, but couldn't time the ball. We had lunch. Simon came over and said that he'd asked Peter Sainsbury how it was going, and he'd said that he hadn't seen anything special yet.

Soon after we'd begun the afternoon session, Simon came marching over to the nets fully padded up and wearing a helmet, the first time I'd seen him do such a thing. I quickly realised why. Following him was the tall, whip-thin, mustachioed figure of Hampshire's opening bowler Steve Malone, known universally as Piggy after a character in a *Two Ronnies* sketch. They took the net next to ours. Piggy marked out his run. He hadn't been picked in the first team for some reason or other and he wasn't happy. With Peter Sainsbury watching out of the corner of his eye, Piggy worked up a real head of steam, fast and hostile.

I had a ringside seat, batting in the next-door net. I could hear the ball cleave the air with a high-frequency buzz. The weather was good, the wickets were hard and Piggy was getting some bounce as well as pace. When he got past the bat, the ball sounded like it was hitting a chain-link fence rather than the soft mesh of the netting. Simon bobbed and weaved as Piggy cranked up. When he did put bat on ball it left his blade with a bright, sharp crack.

Then my dad, in the grip of misplaced ambition and perhaps sensing that the day was slipping away from me, suggested to Peter Sainsbury that Simon and I swap nets. Sainsbury agreed, with a slim smile. I couldn't believe it.

We changed nets. Piggy was unamused by this development. He ran in, breathing fire and grunting as he let it go. He probably bowled no more than nine or ten deliveries, but it seemed like a lot more. He was by some distance the fastest bowler I had ever faced. In fact he was the fastest bowler I'd ever seen up close. He pinned me. The balls I couldn't leave I played from about an inch in front of the stumps. The net I had just left seemed like another country, a distant memory from a happier time. His pace had an actual physical effect on the nervous system: it was like the moment between cutting your finger with a sharp kitchen knife and seeing the blood well up from the wound. The pain doesn't hit right away; instead it waits for the brain to realise that the cut has been made.

Under the sun of a Southampton afternoon, I learned about the gap that separated me from the real game. The real game was a different one from the one that I played. It was as if I was standing in the foothills of a great mountain and had just caught sight of its shimmering face still miles away, hazardous and sheer and unapproachable.

It was over right then. The dream had died in a quiet net by the car park next to the grandstand.

The Day of the Pig.

The day, the end.

The great football manager José Mourinho apparently has a seven-point plan for winning big matches:

1. The game is won by the team that commits fewer errors.
2. Football favours the team that provokes more errors in the opposition.
3. In away matches it's better to encourage mistakes than to try and be superior to the opposition.
4. Whoever has the ball is more likely to make a mistake.
5. Whoever renounces possession reduces the possibility of mistakes.
6. Whoever has the ball has fear.
7. Whoever does not is thereby stronger.

Translated to cricket, it's a good representation of the mindset I had, and I suspect that of many others, too. Cricket's psychological domain, like that of most sports, has become awash with metaphysical mind-coaches and positive thinking, yet here is one of football's biggest winners establishing his philosophy as essentially the opposite of that: 'Whoever has the ball has fear'. It's also an almost perfect representation of what batting had been for two hundred years – don't make the first mistake. Wait for the bowler to make theirs.

Peter Roebuck, the Somerset batsman who had debuted for the county second XI when he was 13 years old and 4ft 2in tall, began a writing career while he was still playing, in part, it seemed, to get some of this off his chest. I carried a couple of his books around in my cricket bag. Sometimes before a game I'd sit in the dressing-room and read his piece in *Tangled Up In White* about Dean Jones's 210 for Australia against India in Chennai, which Roebuck sketched, unforgettably, through the conditions (a nuclear sun, its microwave heat), fragments of dialogue (Jones' batting partner Allan Border: 'quit if you want, we'll get a Queenslander out here') and harrowing notes on Jones' physical and mental deterioration during his innings and afterwards (dry heaves, urinating at the crease, hallucinating in the shower, on a drip at the hospital). Jones' suffering and his mighty courage somehow soothed me, closed the door on self-doubt for a while. It offered any batsman a context for what they did, even if it was only facing the local quicks in a league game.

But the connection to Roebuck – or at least to his writing – went deeper for me. I had another book of his, too. It was called *It Never Rains*, and took the form of a diary of his 1983 season with Somerset. It was the first cricket book I'd read that was equivocal about the game, that made it okay to feel ambiguous about something that dominated your life. It was self-aware, knowing; courageous in its way. Roebuck found cricket and his efforts at playing it funny, ridiculous, poignant, hubristic, bathetic in the sense that it switched from the everyday to the unrepeatable, and slightly, darkly heroic, too.

The start of Somerset's season is beset by rain, endless and total, which sends Roebuck indoors for hours and hours on the bowling machine. His confidence grows and grows until he strides out for his first innings of the year and lasts one ball. As the summer reaches its height, he is gripped by a spiralling six-week depression that concludes on the first day of August with the simple words, 'no entry'. It's a book full of such cadences, the rhythms of real life. There are the identikit ring roads and fuming pub grub of the touring pro, the grinding tyranny of the fixture list, the recognition of unfathomable talent far out of reach (Ian Botham, Viv Richards and Joel Garner are perched in their corners of the Somerset dressing-room), and the comforting quirkiness of any team, anywhere (Colin Dredge, the Demon of Frome and purveyor of deadly induckers, Dasher Denning, the manic, fidgeting opener and so on).

What meant the most to me, though, were the passages where Roebuck heard that he might be considered for England, and began to realise, down in his heart, that he didn't really want to be, or at least that he was profoundly uncertain about it. That admission, and his honesty in revealing it, rounded the game out for me, completed it in my head. This was why cricket was great – because it was not easy. Somehow, the joy of it was increased by this. Whether you played it, wrote about it, thought about it, lived it or watched the odd highlights programme when there was nothing else on, you could never exhaust it. It was, and always would be, too rich, too human and complex, for that. For all of its demanding technicalities and the physiological functions that it pushed to their limits, its real genius was its psychological hinterland, where everyone who played had to live and where everyone lived differently.

Here, the currency was failure and everyone lived with that. Most cricketers failed most of the time. The finest of bowlers might take a wicket, on average, with one ball in sixty. The best batsmen would, statistically, fail to make their career average score in two out of every three innings. The majority of the many millions of deliveries sent down in organised cricket across the centuries resulted in absolutely nothing: no wicket taken, no run scored: stalemate; failure on both sides.

Geoffrey Boycott played his ninety-sixth Test match for England against West Indies at Bridgetown, Barbados, in March 1981. He had been a Test cricketer for 17 years and a professional cricketer since 1962. He had passed Len Hutton's total of 129 first-class centuries, had averaged more than fifty for 11 seasons in a row, and was approaching eight thousand runs in Test matches, at the time more than anyone except Garfield Sobers (who he would pass a year later). He was 40 years old and had been made an OBE in the 1980 New Year's Honours list. He walked out to open the batting against Michael Holding, and faced what many now consider to be one of the fastest overs ever delivered. With the sixth and final ball, Holding bowled Boycott for a duck. In his diary that night, Boycott wrote: 'For the first time in my life, I can look at a scoreboard with a duck against my name and not feel a profound sense of failure.'

What is amazing about that sentence is not just Boycott's recognition of the cumulative force of Holding's over, but the fact that he was still so affected by not scoring runs. He could brood for days over a poor dismissal, running it over and over in his mind. All of his successes could not release him from its grip. It was a fear deeply ingrained in both his personality and his batting. His ruthless single-mindedness was legendary and his desire to avoid failure was at the heart of his batting. Raymond Illingworth, who along with Boycott, Brian Close and Fred Trueman made up what was then the quartet of Greatest Living Yorkshiremen, said of him: 'in technical terms, Geoffrey Boycott is the best batsman in the world today. His problem is his own insecurity. He's never trusted people and I think that facet of his personality comes out in his batting style.'

Rodney Cass, a team-mate in Yorkshire's second XI when Boycott was first trying to make his way in the game, remembered him 'sobbing his heart out' when he was dismissed by bowling faster than anything he'd faced before (perhaps I should have considered crying after facing Steve Malone). As he began to gain a reputation for selfishness in his batting and for self-protection while running between the wickets, he admitted, 'for a long time I found it very difficult to discuss getting out with anybody. I used to go very quiet, into my shell. Basically it was because I felt shame.' Boycott even admitted that he avoided marriage for so long in his life because he was terrified it would fail, and 'I cannot bear failure'.

It was just one example of the game bearing down on a particular personality. Boycott is, I'd guess, a textbook introvert. His biographer Leo McKinstry wrote of him, 'few men have ever been more at ease in solitude or less anxious about loneliness'. Out there in cricket's vast hinterland was the perfect place for him, and for lots of us, because the batsman is always ultimately alone.

The kind of failure that bothered Geoffrey Boycott was quotidian. His playing career and his subsequent life as a commentator and personality have been outstanding successes by almost any measure (and he's now happily married). In all, he went to the wicket 1,316 times with 206 of those ending in not outs. Thus he was dismissed 1,110 times, which is a lot of failure to contend with if he took them all equally hard (he didn't, of course – I once watched him bat in a John Player Sunday League game at May's Bounty. He scored about twenty before lifting one to cover, a most un-Boycott-like shot. He strolled off philosophically and then sat on the balcony writing a letter.).

In David Frith's obituary of Peter Roebuck, he described his stooped batting stance as looking like 'a question mark at the crease', an appropriate metaphor for his cricketing life. He had been ambiguous about the game while he was playing it. He was a brave player – opening batsmen have to be. But three years after he published *It Never Rains*, he became caught up in one of English domestic cricket's most divisive moments, an event that would induce a paranoia that shadowed the rest of his life. In 1986, at the end of his first season as Somerset captain, he was instrumental in persuading the county not to renew the contracts of its two great overseas stars Viv Richards and Joel Garner. Ian Botham, who was Richards' closest

friend, called Roebuck 'Judas' and left the county in pro-
test. Intellectually, Roebuck knew he was right. Although
the mighty triumvirate had turned Somerset into a quixotic and dazzling force, Taunton packed and agog at their
brilliance, they were in decline. Somerset had not won a
trophy since 1983, and had finished bottom and then second bottom of the championship in their last two seasons.
But there was more to it than intellect. In *It Never Rains*
Roebuck made it clear that he felt the three were separated from him by their talent. They existed in another
orbit, apparently free from the anxieties that beset lesser
mortals. County cricket was easy for them, a nice way to
spend a summer. Other things came easily, too. They were
dressing-room naturals, charismatic men to whom others
gravitated, classic examples of the 'women want them and
men want to be them' school. Roebuck was different, academically gifted (he had a first in law from Cambridge),
sharp-tongued, intense, socially awkward, intolerant of
sloppiness. His hero was the eccentric pedagogue R. J.
O. 'Boss' Meyer, his headmaster at Millfield School and a
former Somerset captain himself.*

And as Matthew Engel, a former editor of *Wisden* and
a former friend of Roebuck, would write: 'the cricketing
community largely assumed that he was homosexual and
attracted to young men, but also very repressed.'

---

*Roebuck's interview at Millfield was in itself extraordinary. One of Meyer's
favourite tricks for any potential student of a cricketing bent was to throw an
orange at them as they entered the room. Roebuck caught it. By the interview's end, Roebuck not only had his place, but Meyer had offered both his
parents jobs at the school.

It's hard to imagine a man less like Botham or Richards, and yet they had ten years of friendship, in which, as the Somerset spinner turned journalist and commentator Vic Marks recalled, 'they would have preposterous, noisy arguments about anything, with Roebuck's forensic skills matched by Botham's bombast'. Roebuck even co-authored a book with Botham. Yet the split, when it came, was irrevocable and, for Roebuck, deadly.

'What I lacked,' Roebuck wrote in *It Never Rains*, 'was that sardonic sense of humour which offers a shield against the severest blows.'

He replaced Richards and Garner with the stellar New Zealand batsman Martin Crowe and a young Steve Waugh, and Somerset improved steadily over the next few seasons. By 1989, Roebuck was once again a contender for an England place, possibly as 'the new Brearley' – opening bat, captain and resident sage. He was taken to Holland to captain an England team in two unofficial games. One was (shockingly) lost, and afterwards Micky Stewart, who was managing the side, told the journalists following the tour to ignore everything Roebuck had said in his press conference. The people who counted had taken against him, and the call never came.

Two years later he retired. His bitterness towards England showed when he took out Australian citizenship ('nothing would rile him more [after that] than to be described as an Englishman', wrote his colleague Malcolm Knox) and became a radio commentator and waspish cricket columnist for the *Sydney Morning Herald*, where his writing was often brilliant, sometimes caustic but rarely had the elegiac melancholy of *It Never Rains* or *Tangled Up In White*. It perhaps reflected his anger at self-imposed exile and at his enemies, real and imagined. He kept a house in the West Country and returned to captain Devon in the Minor Counties Championship, some of his happiest cricketing times. In 1999, while covering a series between South Africa and Zimbabwe in Harare, he met a 16-year-old boy called Psychology Maziwisa who was living in a home for orphans and destitute children. He would become the first of Roebuck's African 'sons'. Through a trust that he helped to establish and later with his own money – half a million dollars, Maziwisa estimated – Roebuck provided a tertiary education for dozens of boys. That same year he brought three promising cricketers from South Africa, all aged 19, to his home in England to advance their game. He warned them beforehand that he would use corporal punishment to discipline them if they broke 'house rules'. In 2001, he pleaded guilty to three counts of common assault for striking the men on the buttocks with a cricket bat, and received a four-month suspended jail sentence. It further weakened and complicated his attachment to England.

He purchased a block of land near Pietermaritzburg and built Straw Hat Farm where he spent part of the year with Maziwisa and as many as 12 other students. He was living a role that was perhaps to him laid down by his hero R. J. O. Meyer. In 2010, Roebuck moved himself and the boys to a ten-bedroom house called Sunshine near Pietermaritzburg University. Away from Africa he lived an ascetic and austere life and used almost all of his money to support his students.

On 12 November 2011, he went to cover the final morning of the Test between South Africa and Australia at Newlands, a mad game in which Australia had bowled South Africa out for 96 and then been dismissed themselves for 47. At breakfast he spoke to Allan Border, the former Australian captain, about the team's plight. Once the match concluded with a South African victory, he filed his copy and had lunch with Tony Irish of the South African Cricketers' Association. He chatted to his friend Jim Maxwell of the ABC, and returned to his hotel, the Southern Sun. He was visited there by South African police, who questioned him over an alleged sexual assault on a 26-year-old student called Itai Gondo. Roebuck returned to his room on the sixth floor of the hotel with a uniformed officer in order to change his clothes. From there he rang Jim Maxwell and asked him to call a lawyer and then come to his room. Minutes later he was dead, having apparently jumped from the window.

In 2001, Roebuck had provided the foreword to an edition of David Frith's *Silence of the Heart*, his book about cricketing suicides. 'Some people have predicted a gloomy end for this writer,' he wrote. 'One former colleague said so to my face in September 1986. It will not be so. The art is to find other things that matter just as much as cricket, which stretch you just as far.'

Scott Boswell's penultimate over as a professional cricketer was witnessed by a full house at Lord's and subsequently by more than one and a half million people on YouTube, where it's available under the title, 'the worst over ever?'

He was 26 years old and playing for Leicestershire against Somerset in the final of the C&G Trophy. He had been the star of Leicester's semi-final win over Lancashire, taking four for 44, every wicket an England player. The final was going to be the best day of his sporting life.

He got his first over out of the way, always a hurdle for the nervous cricketer. Peter Bowler cut him to the boundary, but apart from that the ball came out okay. Bowler nudged the second delivery of his next for a single, which gave the strike to Marcus Trescothick. Then it began, the voice in his head that told him he struggled bowling to left-handers. When he looked up again, Trescothick appeared to be nothing more than a dot 'fifty yards away . . . I just couldn't see him. Then I bowled a wide and I heard the noise of the crowd. I bowled a second wide and the noise got louder and louder and louder.'

It was like something out of a nightmare, only this was real. He began to sweat. He felt himself gripping the ball too tightly. He just wanted to get it over with, so he started to rush everything. The famous Lord's slope threw him off his run. He swapped to round the wicket but the wides kept coming, five in a row at one point, some of them miles down the leg side, others miles down the off. When he did get one straight, Trescothick belted it to the boundary. 'Keep bowling,' said the umpire George Sharp out of the side of his mouth. In all the over lasted for seven minutes, 14 deliveries and to Scott Boswell it has in a way never ended.

The crowd crowed at him. He messed up a piece of fielding soon afterwards and the crowd got even worse.

'Bring on the Boswell . . . Bring on the Boswell . . .' they chanted.

Leicester lost the game. The next match was against Gloucestershire. No one came and told him he wasn't playing – they didn't have to. No one spoke to him at all, except one team-mate, Jimmy Ormond, who took him for a pint and asked what had happened. Boswell didn't know. He got hundreds of emails, some of them accusing him of match-fixing. Two weeks later, Leicester told him that his contract was not being renewed. There was one more Sunday League fixture, against Nottinghamshire, a vital one that if Leicester won would give them the title. He agreed to play but before the game found himself breaking down in a shop near the ground. He bowled one over, which began with a wide and cost 18 runs, and then he pretended to have cramp and walked off the field.

It took Scott Boswell a decade to rebuild his relationship with the game that had dominated his life. He started work as a salesman and was offered a chance to play as a professional for a club side but even then he couldn't stop bowling wides. He became depressed, began drinking, put on weight. He played club cricket as a batsman only. His wife took a life-coaching course and taught him about positive thinking. He trained as a teacher and his confidence grew. One day, his captain forced him to come on and bowl in a second XI club match. The over went on and on, for 27 deliveries, but with his twenty-eighth he bowled a straight one and got an lbw. He collapsed on the pitch in tears. After that, his bowling came back. The club reached the final of the Village Cup, which is played each year at Lord's. He returned to the scene of his downfall as twelfth man and had to go on and field. 'Bloody hell, I was holding back some tears,' he said, but at last he was redeemed.

★

What happened to Scott Boswell during that C&G final? How can it be explained? He had spent almost his entire life bowling a cricket ball, ever since he was a little kid, and he had always been able to do it. Suddenly he couldn't do it any more. All he could think of was that his form had dropped off a little between the semi-final and the final. He knew that the club were unsure about picking him. In the team meeting the night before the game, a coach told him 'not to fuck up'. The insecurity got to him, and somehow the sight of Marcus Trescothick triggered a negative state of mind so destructive that he was unable to do something he'd been doing successfully for his whole time on earth.

It had happened to others too, albeit not as publicly. Keith Medlycott was a left-arm spinner good enough to be selected to tour the West Indies with England in 1990. He was in Sri Lanka for an England A team tour the following winter, bowling to Mark Ramprakash in the nets. He sent down a full toss that Ramprakash smashed somewhere into next week, and everything changed. By the end of the following English season, a man who had taken 357 first-class wickets for Surrey couldn't let go of the ball and retired. He was 26, the same age as Scott Boswell had been on that day at Lord's. For some reason, left-arm spinners seemed especially vulnerable: Phil Edmonds, never a man known for lacking confidence, had to overcome an episode by limiting his run-up to a single stride. Fred Swarbrook, a tweaker beloved of Derbyshire fans for his bald pate and generous waistline, suddenly began sending down head-high full tosses. A faith healer told him to keep a lucky pebble in his pocket, but the first time he did, he let one go so early it lobbed gently upwards and landed on his head.

'Stick the ball in your pocket and bowl the pebble,' said his skipper Eddie Barlow.

The Lancashire spinner Simon Kerrigan suffered a day almost as dreadful as Scott Boswell's when he was selected for England in an Ashes Test at The Oval in 2013. The seamer Chris Woakes also debuted, and bowled an innocuous opening spell in which Shane Watson took him for five boundaries. Watson was a player often buffeted by fortune himself, but on his day he could be destructive. Alastair Cook hoicked Woakes from the attack and brought Kerrigan on to bowl in tandem with England's established spinner Graeme Swann. Watson had already smashed Swann into the stands when Kerrigan trotted up to bowl his first ball in Test cricket. His nerves must have been compounded by the man he was bowling to: in a tour game against England Lions the week before the Test, Watson had hit him for seven fours and a six in a few overs. His third delivery was a full toss that Watson swiped to the boundary. His fifth went through midwicket for another. His next over was spectacularly bad. A horribly slow drag-down was cannoned through midwicket by Watson, who walked down the wicket to the next and lofted it straight for another boundary. The next three were all short: Watson cut the first for two and slaughtered the other two through midwicket. Kerrigan looked like a man whose muscles had frozen up. The ball was looping gently from his hand with no help from his body or his front arm. Cook took him off immediately with figures of 2-0-28-0. He didn't bowl again until just before tea, when his next two overs included more half-trackers and a head-high full toss. In all, he bowled eight overs in Australia's first innings, none at all in their second and has never been selected again. As the former Indian international Aakash Chopra observed, a man who had sent down more than nine thousand deliveries in first-class cricket and taken 164 wickets ended up bowling slow long-hops and chin-high full tosses, his lifelong dream turned living nightmare in the space of 12 deliveries. It was very probably the worst he had bowled anywhere at any point in his life. Why?

Kerrigan and Woakes had been last-minute selections – so late that Ian Botham was only asked shortly before the toss to undertake the traditional cap-presentation ceremony for debutants. Australia had expected England to recall Chris Tremlett, who had bowled some devastating spells in the 3-1 Ashes win in Australia in 2010–11. The fact that he wasn't filled them with glee: Watson admitted as much at the end of the day's play – 'I wasn't complaining . . .'

'You are exposed out there,' he went on to say of Kerrigan. 'You could definitely sense he was nervous especially after those first couple of overs.'

It didn't just happen to left-arm spinners though. The Yorkshire and England all-rounder Gavin Hamilton broke down to the extent that he delivered five wides in an over in a game against Sussex and asked his captain to take him off. Hampshire pace bowler Kevin Emery took 83 wickets in the 1982 season, was voted the county's Young Cricketer of the Year and then lost his ability to bowl in what was described as 'one of Hampshire cricket's greatest mysteries'. David Gurr, a quick bowler of some potential, was contending for a place in a Somerset side that contained Botham and Garner when a lack of confidence bled into his action and he couldn't stop bowling wides. He retired to work in life assurance.

What was clear was that the affliction was psychological rather than physical. It affected bowlers rather than batsmen because they repeated a single action rather than a variety of shots, and also because their first mistake was not fatal; it did not exclude them from the game. By the time that Hamilton and Boswell were afflicted, the condition was being termed the yips, a steal from golf, where it was used to describe the mysterious and sudden loss of the ability to putt. It had its equivalents in snooker too, where the multiple world champion Stephen Hendry had been affected, and in darts, where the great Eric Bristow found himself unable to let go of his arrows and christened it 'dart-itis'.

Mark Bawden was a promising bowler who found at the age of 16 that he couldn't let go of the ball and so he studied sports science and then psychology, wrote his doctorate on the yips and went on to work with the English Institute of Sport and the England cricket team. He identified some common factors in suffering bowlers: the feeling of a subconscious action becoming an uncomfortably conscious one; the batsman appearing to be sixty yards away rather than twenty; a massive decrease in confidence and self-belief. 'We've found out that it happens in multiple sports and that it's an emotional problem, unrelated to sport, that manifests as a physical thing when you're under pressure,' he says.

But there were differences, too. Simon Kerrigan returned to Lancashire and continued to bowl successfully in the county game. Gavin Hamilton gave up bowling but made an ODI century for his native Scotland against Ireland and went on to captain his country. Scott Boswell is making his way back as a coach.

In the end, Bawden said, 'all of the actions of a cricket match become psychological triggers. You have to strip them away and start again . . . The yips can come back. They tend to be fairly ingrained.'

In *Fever Pitch*, his book about male obsession and football fandom, Nick Hornby writes about an Arsenal player called Gus Caesar. Gus was playing at the time I used to go and watch Arsenal. He was behind other defenders like David O'Leary, Viv Anderson, Tony Adams and Steve Bould in the pecking order, and seemed to make most of his appearances as a sub or when injury struck. Gus was a crowd favourite but not in the way that the others were, for their warrior-like qualities. In the 1988 League Cup final he'd made a catastrophic error that allowed Luton Town to equalise at 2-2 and they went on to an against-the-odds win. He was voted the worst Arsenal player ever by the club's most popular fanzine *The Gooner*, and came in at number three in a poll by *The Times* to find the 50 worst players to appear in the English First Division.

To me Gus seemed unlucky. He usually played when things were going badly, and because he was nervous he'd rush his clearances and shank them into the stands, and the crowd would start their ironic cheers. In *Fever Pitch* he emerges as a strange kind of hero. Hornby observes that Gus began as the best footballer in his street, and then in his class and then in his school. He went on to be the best footballer in his district, the best at his trials and then the best in the age-group teams at Arsenal. Of all of the kids who began to make their way in the game, Gus was one of the few that were offered professional forms, and one of the few of those that actually got through the reserve games and into the first team. Not only that, he played three times for the England Under-21 side, and more than fifty times for Arsenal, and still all that anyone talked about was that game against Luton Town and how bad he was. Even people who had never seen him play used to go on with mock authority about him.

'Gus Caesar clearly had more talent than nearly every-one of his generation and it still wasn't quite enough,' Nick Hornby wrote. '. . . Gus must have known he was good, just as any pop band who has ever played the Marquee know they are destined for Madison Square Garden and an *NME* front cover, and just as any writer who has sent off a completed manuscript to Faber and Faber knows that he is two years away from the Booker. You trust that feeling with your life, you feel the strength and deter-mination it gives you coursing through your veins like heroin . . . and it doesn't mean anything at all.'

For me, failure, in the end, wasn't hard to accept. After the Day of the Pig, Peter Sainsbury didn't ring, and I was secretly glad that he hadn't. The emotions that facing Steve Malone provoked were complicated, but I some-how understood what they meant. First was the shock. Malone's pace had shrunk my world down to almost nothing. Just as things telescoped for bowlers suffering from the yips and the batsman looked like he was sixty yards away, so Steve Malone appeared as the opposite to me, a man magnified to such an extent he filled the entire lens of my view. I thought of facing him out in the middle, surrounded by the slip cordon and a short leg, having not just to survive but to score runs. It seemed unimaginable. And this was Steve Malone, a man who couldn't get into the Hampshire team because they had other better, quicker bowlers like Malcolm Marshall, who was not only much faster, he could move the ball late through the air and off the wicket.* And every county seemed to have one (or more): Wayne Daniel at Middlesex, Sylvester Clarke at Surrey, Mike Procter at Gloucester, Imran Khan and Garth Le Roux at Sussex, Garner and Botham at Somerset, Bob Willis at Warwickshire, Clive Rice and Richard Hadlee at Nottinghamshire and so on. There were people out there who could do extraordinary things, who could bowl even faster than Steve Malone, and others who could face it, day after day, month after month, year upon year, at least until time and life wore them down.

---

*When I was about 14 I faced two deliveries from Malcolm Marshall, which he bowled from a couple of paces at an indoor net in Basingstoke. It was run by Tim Tremlett, father of Chris and a fine Hampshire seam bowler himself, and I can only presume that the then young Marshall had dropped by to say hello. He bowled a few at all of us, just so we could say we'd faced him. He lobbed the first down gently and I played a rather showy cover drive (I always was at my best in the nets . . .). I barely saw the second, which appeared, in a hazy red blur, to swing out, swing back in again, bounce and almost strike me a killer blow in the nether regions before smacking into the back of the canvas. Naturally, everyone there found it hilarious (except for me). Suffice to say I never again tried to cover drive Malcolm Marshall. To have faced the great man, even in those circumstances, remains one of my proudest moments.

Maybe, after lots of exposure, I could have got more used to Steve Malone's pace. Simon had been able to play against him, and I'd played enough with Simon to know that I could at least hang in there with him at times. But then Simon was the star batsman in any team he played in, and for Hampshire seconds he batted at number eight or nine. I thought of the time that Barry Richards came and played at Fleet. Batting against Dinger Bell had been as simple for him as batting against my sister was for me.

It was a divide that could not be crossed even if I'd wanted to cross it. And the truth was that I didn't. Like Peter Roebuck in 1983, what I really felt when the call didn't come was relief. It wasn't just the realisation of the magnitude of talent in the game and the gaps it created. It was about pressure and desire. Simon threw himself into the game without doubt – I'm sure he had some but his desire to compete overwhelmed everything else. I realised somewhere in my 16-year-old brain that I didn't want to put myself through the endless uncertainty, the constant worry, the fear of failure. I understood that the game's hinterland was vast and powerful and potentially destructive. I wasn't good enough, and I was grateful for the proof, grateful for the Pig.

Mourinho's rule six: whoever has the ball has fear.

Mourinho's rule seven: whoever does not is thereby stronger.

The Day of the Pig.

The beginning and the end.

5
Amateurs

It's one of the great beauties of cricket that a team game can sustain mad, glorious and destructive personal ambition. This thought came to me when I watched Chris Gayle hit the first ball of a Test match for six, because I once played with a man whose desire was to hit the first ball of a match for six, too. That simple dream had gripped his soul and would not let go.

This was back in the days when bats were slim and sixes were rare currency. I was 13 or 14, just starting to play senior cricket along with age-group games at Wrecclesham CC. We'll call him Pete, because that was his name, a lovely man in love with the game. After thirty-odd years at the crease, he was still to make a fifty, in part due to the relentless pursuit of his goal.

He opened the batting because he'd been at the club for as long as anyone, and because there was no man there who wanted to deny him his chance. It was made tougher because it was dependent on us batting first, so sometimes he would go weeks without getting the opportunity. But when it came, well . . . Pete died often, but he never died wondering. He heaved at every first ball he ever received, short or full, wide or straight, good or bad. I would imagine he got more golden ducks than any other opener in the country, but he never adjusted his game, never thought, 'I'll just bat and try and get that fifty', never allowed reason to crush that pure and perfect vision of a bowler running in as the clock hit one, all heads turning upwards as a new red ball sailed into the endless sky.

He never did it, or at least not to my knowledge. But he did get his fifty. It came in an in-house game, when our Under-17 side played the first XI one hazy Sunday afternoon. We had some good players in that Under-17 team, including a couple of very decent opening bowlers. They batted. Pete carved at the first ball, which missed everything. Then he carved at all the others, and miraculously it came off. Balls fell wide of fielders, edges went for four. He even middled a few, and he was a big, strong guy. Finally he swung, connected once again and the applause came up from the pavilion.

'Twenty-five years I've waited for that,' he yelled, his bat held high above his head, his face split by a grin that said every moment of the wait had been worthwhile. He was out next ball.

The single most remarkable piece of cricket gear I have ever seen resided in the bottom of the club kitbag at Wrecclesham. The concept of the club kitbag no longer exists, but back then most sides had a couple of guys who weren't bothered about owning equipment of their own and who were happy to delve around in the club bag for a pair of mismatched pads, some sweat-stained gloves, maybe a mildewed thigh pad that they could use and then chuck back in at the end of the day. No one ever cleaned it out, or even touched it unless they had to. Instead it remained locked in the dressing-room at the end of each weekend, and probably right through the winter, too.

Within this particular bag, it lay. A stitched-in manufacturer's label described it as an 'abdominal guard' but that hardly did it justice. It looked like something Henry VIII wore to the jousting, a great tin codpiece attached to a wide, padded V-shaped belt that had to be stepped into like a jockstrap and then secured around the waist with a couple of long ties.

It was known as 'Cyril's Box' after the only player who would (or could) wear it, the first-team wicketkeeper Cyril. He was a remarkable man, mid-fifties, squat, powerful, with giant, hooked hands apparently impervious to pain. I never discovered what it was that Cyril did, but it was some kind of hard physical labour that had produced both great strength and admirable stoicism. He barely ever said anything; just turned up in the dressing-room every Saturday, stripped off his street clothes, retrieved the box from wherever he had thrown it the week before, strapped himself in, pulled the rest of his gear over it and walked out onto the pitch.

Like Rod Marsh, Cyril had iron gloves. The ball often used to fly off them at tremendous speed, accompanied on crucial occasions by a muttered oath. He'd sometimes stand up to the opening bowlers, usually without explanation, and it was then that the abdominal guard earned its corn. The ball would smack Cyril in the vital area, and then ricochet away with a metallic clang. On one famous occasion, a batsman was caught at second slip direct from Cyril's box and the game took a while to restart: several people were actually crying with laughter. After a match, Cyril would silently remove it, sometimes pushing out a dent with a thick thumb. He'd get changed back into his street clothes and then wander up to the pub, his love for the game expressed perfectly and eloquently in the slow satisfaction of his walk.

At Wrecclesham, with its windswept, sloping field, I was inducted into the world of amateur cricket, and into the world of men. They played cricket for what seemed to me obscure reasons. They weren't any good at it, so what were they doing? What did Pete get out of being dismissed for nought each week? What drove Cyril to devote his Saturday afternoons off to crouching behind the sticks? I didn't get it, couldn't see it. They seemed to find everything funny, but I didn't understand half of their jokes. Some of the players often couldn't wait for the game to end so that they could go to the pub.

One day Pete let me open the batting with a guy who'd played for some years but then moved away. Everyone had been anticipating his return with great glee and excitement – they all seemed to love him. I don't remember his name now, but when he turned up he was small and manic, a real fast-twitch fibre kind of bloke. He cracked jokes constantly. He seemed quite put out to be opening with a kid and immediately tried to flay the bowling, yelling for runs every time he connected. After a couple of overs he hit one straight to a fielder. When I looked up he was almost next to me.

'Run . . . run . . .' he screamed.

I took a couple of steps towards him but instinct kept my bat grounded behind the crease line. We were still a few yards apart when the stumps at the far end were broken.

'You're out . . .' he said to me.

I knew that I wasn't.

'No, you didn't cross,' said one of the fielders. 'It's you, not him.'

He stood in the middle of the pitch staring at the umpire, who eventually gave him out.

'Well,' he shouted, turning back to me. 'If you're fucking staying, fucking well get on with it . . .' He stomped off. Pete came out at number three (we were batting last, so the first-ball six was off the agenda for another week).

'Don't take any notice of him,' he said, kindly. But I was shocked by it. My life had been so sheltered I don't think I'd ever been shouted at by an adult like that. I stayed in mainly because I was afraid to get out, but when I did and walked fearfully back to the pavilion, I discovered he'd got in his car and gone home.

I've been involved in plenty of run-outs since, and, as a general rule, emotionally it's better to be the one run out – the karmic points bank up; it's guilt-free and vaguely tragic and doesn't usually affect selection. There are certainly a few that went the other way that I feel genuinely sorrowful about. But that day at Wrecclesham is the one run-out that has stayed with me, even though everyone else present almost certainly forgot it many years ago.

Sheer human variety has shaped my experience of amateur cricketers. In other words, I've seen it all – probably. The slip catch missed because the fielder was on ecstasy.

The batting partner who sidled up the pitch between overs and said, 'watch out for my calling – I took two lines of cocaine last night and I'm still feeling jumpy . . .'. The bat fetishists, the casual larceny (I was once given leg before by the opposition's ancient umpire to a ball going miles down the leg-side. They'd gone up in a vociferous and ludicrous appeal, and as I walked off their captain said to me, 'Bad luck, he always gives those . . .'), the ersatz pros (these men are especially prone to behaviour picked up from televised cricket. Since the introduction of the stump mic and the proliferation of professional jargon in the commentary box, it's now rare to play in a game and not hear about 'wheels' and 'gas', 'decking' and 'hooping' and 'ragging'. One guy kept calling the umpire 'umpy' . . .), the tantrum throwers, the guys that are never out and are still talking about their 'duff' decision hours later, usually with a kind of faux bewilderment. My all-time favourite excuse comes from my friend and teammate Nicholas Hogg, an estimable cricketer, who once claimed he hadn't batted well because he'd 'been looking for a flat all week'.

The captain's lot is usually the worst as he is dealing with the horrors of trying to get 11 men out on the field (there's almost always a last-minute cry off, often connected to not having told a significant other of the plan to play) – one skipper I know has filled his team by walking up to people in the supermarket and asking if they want a game.

Amateur cricket, at its lower levels at least, floats on the delusions of all of us who play. We are in love with an idea of ourselves that perhaps never existed, or, if it did, it did so only fleetingly and many years ago. There is something about the game's eternal renewals that promises that one day – perhaps this day – will be *our* day, the one where everything that we think we are, we become. It's madness. For a while I followed a wonderful blog written pseudonymously by 'Tom Redfern' (a sly steal – Redfern was the man at the other end when A. E. J. Collins made the last few of his 628 not out). It was about his quest to score a maiden hundred. He didn't want his first to be anything other than perfect, or at least perfect for him. It had to be made, in his words, 'against cricketers who rate themselves; against players who think they are better than you. It must come in less than fifty balls.' Tom could play. He went to Millichamp & Hall and got a custom-made bat. Each week, he posted videos of his innings on the blog. He often got starts, even against good bowling, and a few times he passed fifty, but the feat eluded him. Fifty-ball centuries are tough for professional players. In my years of playing I think I've been on the field for one or two. Tom was like Ahab seeking his whale. He was doomed. It was magnificent in its way. We exchanged a few messages. I told him he was too good a player not to have made a ton, and that he should forget about the number of balls it took and just enjoy scoring one. He rejected that argument entirely, and I admired him for it.

At Basingstoke, a batsman called Dave Hacker, with whom I occasionally opened in the Under-17s, once scored five hundreds in a row out on the Bounty, each majestic. His attempt at a sixth wasn't bad either. He made seventy-odd before the run ended. It was amazing to watch something just click in the mind of a talented sportsman.

Dave had a moment of realisation and understanding and allowed himself to go with it (soon afterwards he gave up cricket for hockey, and I believe became an international). Perhaps the strangest innings I was a part of came in an Under-17 game when Bill the groundsman cut a pitch on the very edge of the square, leaving a boundary of about thirty yards. A guy called Rob Eustace had the day of his life and kept bunting the ball into the car park. We put on more than two hundred together, of which I scored less than fifty. He got on strike on that short side and by the end of our innings he'd made a double-century, still the only one I've ever seen scored in an amateur game.

Amateur cricket's dramas are small-scale and domestic. It deals with indignity rather than tragedy. It suits the comic writer. Teams that stay together for years become like dysfunctional families, riven by slights and betrayals both real and imagined, huge fights and bluff reconciliations, ancient wounds opened and re-healed, the dressing-room filled with relationships unfathomable to the outsider. Players become as aware of their team-mates' cricketing quirks and habits as they are of their spouses' marital ones. There have been very funny books written about teams like these: Marcus Berkmann's *Rain Men* and Harry Thompson's *Penguins Stopped Play* are wonderful examples of the art – for any player, it's the comedy of recognition.

P. G. Wodehouse was by all accounts tickled to share the nickname 'Plum' with Pelham Warner and named his gentleman's valet Jeeves after the Warwickshire bowler Percy Jeeves, who died during the attack on the High Wood at the Somme in 1916. George Orwell, another cricket fan, thought Wodehouse's 1909 novel *Mike*, which introduced Mike Jackson as the young star of a cricketing family, was his best. His glorious comedy was well suited to the game, and it featured often in his writing until he moved to America when golf, another sport with amateurs ripe for send-up, took over in his affections (Wodehouse even claimed, perhaps tongue in cheek, that he came to like baseball more than cricket because, 'I'd go to see Surrey play, say, Lancashire, and I'd find Lancashire has won the toss, and they'd bat all day, whereas with baseball, the other side only bats about 10 minutes at the most').

There is a wonderful novel called *Chinaman* by the Sri Lankan writer Shehan Karunatilaka that has as its narrator an alcoholic, cynical and ageing cricket journalist nicknamed WG, a man with a long-suffering wife and a drop-out son named after Garfield Sobers. WG is investigating the disappearance of a mercurial mystery spinner called Pradeep Mathew, who, in an echo of Arthur Conan Doyle's famous tale *The Story of Spedegue's Dropper*, can even bowl a double-bouncer that skims down the pitch 'like a pebble across water'.

Yet amateur cricket's artistic metier is not really literature but the sitcom. It fits the format perfectly because it can be used so easily to reveal character and also as a metaphor for class, which is – or at least was – the subject of most sitcoms. *Dad's Army* has a cricket episode called 'The Test' in which Mainwaring's Home Guard take on Warden Hodges' ARP, who are boosted by the recruitment of a tearaway fast bowler played by Fred Trueman. Fiery Fred sustains an injury after bowling a single ball,

Pike gets a duck and Sergeant Wilson – who else – scores a match-winning 81 not out. In *Fawlty Towers*, the hotel's resident Major often references the cricket scores in the newspaper ('Evening, Fawlty, Hampshire won.' 'Did it? Oh isn't that good, how splendid!'), and in the episode 'The Germans' discusses the time he took a 'sprightly looking girl' to see India play at The Oval – 'I must have been keen on her . . . Fine match, a marvellous finish . . .' *The Young Ones* play a violent indoor match in the 'Summer Holiday' episode, which concludes with Vyvyan setting Rik on fire to create 'the Ashes'. Richard Harris adapted his play *Outside Edge*, about a cricket team and their marital problems, into a sitcom that ran for three series in the 1990s.

The most resonant and perfect example of why amateur cricket works in this way comes in *Ever Decreasing Circles*, John Esmonde's sitcom of the early 1980s, the fading final glory years of the genre. *Ever Decreasing Circles*, like *Terry and June*, *The Good Life*, *Brush Strokes*, *Keeping Up Appearances* and many others, featured the nascent middle classes, dwellers in the cul-de-sacs of the seventies boom-burbs: commuters, middle managers, golf club members, with their dreams of conservatories and soufflés and the company dinner-dance. These pretensions were easily speared, but not often as darkly as they were in *Ever Decreasing Circles*.

It's contextual, of course: the show is a thing of its time, but there's a quiet, unacknowledged and deep-running despair to it that in retrospect seems quite daring. Richard Briers plays Martin, a pedantic, obsessive-compulsive valve salesman with a photocopier in his garage and moral code as inflexible as a periodic table. Now, he would reside somewhere on the autism spectrum; back then he was just funny, and not unrepresentative. Most people knew someone like him.

His neighbours were Howard and Hilda, a couple that seem weirder today than they ever did then, a middle-aged, guileless pair who wore matching jumpers and thought the same thoughts at the same time. The jeopardy came from Paul, a new arrival in the close who was handsome, urbane, funny, good at everything, and – most shockingly of all – the owner of a successful hair salon. Martin loathed Paul, of course, not just for who he was, but for what he represented. There was an unsettling subtext, to this. Martin's wife obviously fancied Paul, to which Martin was oblivious (thus making any hint of betrayal all the more devastating).

Ennui, boredom, acceptance, resentment, disillusionment, loyalty were all there, just alluded to rather than highlighted. The set-up for 'The Cricket Match' is classic: like all sitcoms, it telegraphs its ending while allowing it to be savoured. Martin is the skipper of the local team. He has run the side for 14 years, dreaming of promotion to a division where they could play a club that has 'underfloor heating in the dressing rooms' (another impossibly glamorous idyll of the 1970s). He is also the fixtures secretary and the man responsible for looking after the kit, which he has just whitened and varnished (Wrecclesham CC could have done with Martin).

He's desperate to stop Paul playing, of course, because he knows he'll be better than everyone else. The rest of the team all want Paul in, even if it means they can't play themselves. There is a tremendous little scene around this in Martin's garage, where Paul arrives to confirm his availability (he's told he'll still have to fill in and return the postcard that Martin will send to him). Here Martin recalls Denis Compton ('I always get emotional when I think of him'), and Compton's captain at Middlesex, F. G. Mann, 'Not so great a player by many a long chalk,' Martin says, 'but nevertheless his captain. Never ever did you see Denis question FG, slight FG or demean FG.'

'What are you trying to say?' Paul asks, disingenuously.

'I'm not trying to say anything,' says Martin. 'I am saying it.'

The story runs its inevitable course: Paul isn't playing until a bloke called Curly (he's bald, naturally, as all people in sitcoms called Curly are) is injured in the warm-up. The opposition bat first and rack up 200, partly because Martin won't bring Paul on to bowl. In reply, they're 46–7 when Martin is out in ridiculous circumstances, leaving Paul to bat with Howard, a man who, it's revealed, proposed to his wife while stoned on endorphins after making his highest ever score of 11. Paul gets the runs.

There's a sting, though, in the last scene. Martin is in the dressing-room with his wife, avoiding the jollity of the bar, where Paul is holding court. The opposition skipper comes in and announces he won't be accepting Martin's offer of a jug for his lads. 'That bloke who got the runs played for Cambridge University. If you want to win that much, we won't be drinking with you.'

It could have ended there, with Martin proved right. Instead, his wife suggests they go into the bar, where Martin always plays the piano and everyone has a singsong. Just as they go to open the door, the piano starts up.

Martin's wife looks through.

'Yes,' she says, 'it is him . . .'

It's equivocal and bittersweet, and for the time, brilliantly done. The match is equally well observed: it rings with scenes and characters familiar to any club player – bored wives on the boundary, no spikes in the pavilion, the crooked, unchallengeable away umpire. I'd say John Esmonde was a fan: alongside the Compton/Mann scene, Paul walks into bat with a Jumbo, which in the early eighties was the bat *du jour*, used by Graham Gooch and King Viv. Martin makes do with a wafer-thin Duncan Fearnley. The 'action' is badly filmed, another sitcom tradition (the match in *Dad's Army* takes place deep into autumn and apparently on a football pitch). Cricket, though, represented something, and how the characters reacted to it said something about them. No one's used the game in this way for a long time, and it would take a good writer to make it work in these more atomised days.

Occasionally life would imitate art, or at least provide the kind of storyline that seems more believable in a sitcom or a made-for-TV movie. I was once on the field when a bowler took all ten wickets. It happened many seasons ago in a midweek game, one of those that, even when you had nothing else to do, made you feel like you'd bunked off real life for the afternoon. The ground was deep in the countryside somewhere, a natural bowl out in the woods with an erratic boundary line dictated by the encroaching trees. We got changed in a stone hut with a thatched roof set side-on to the wicket. We scattered some plastic chairs outside. The peeling scoreboard still had the numbers from the last game hanging on it; someone was unhooking them and throwing them noisily onto a pile. A single, weathered sightscreen stood at either end.

We bowled first. Simon Lock opened up. He marked his run. He was like a minor character from *Blackadder*, short back and sides in a severe parting, bumfluff pencil 'tache, big old bowling boots that looked like they'd been passed down through generations. He came in with knees pumping, quickish but not rapid – reminiscent of John Arlott's great line about John Easter: 'the slowest fast bowler in England.'

The new cherry sang for him that day. A couple were bowled, I caught one at second slip. We stuck in a short leg and got one there, too. They were four or five down for not very many. A brief stand, then a couple more. By now we had about five slips, gullies, close men, the works. Simon got another: that was eight. Every over from the other end had a strange tension – neither side actually wanted a wicket to go down. At drinks, we half joked about deliberately dropping one if a chance came, but that somehow didn't feel right either. If it was going to happen, it couldn't be manufactured.

Simon did it. The last two, from memory, were bowled. We surrounded him. He was a lovely guy, always great to play with. He deserved it. It had taken maybe an hour and a half. They'd only made sixty-odd and we knocked them off quickly, on the ground surrounded by trees, underneath the perfect sky.

It's a melancholic feeling recalling that day, and the memory of it has a dream-like quality. I wonder what happened to Simon Lock, and to everyone who played.

Have they had good lives since then? I hope so. Nothing ties us except that game, but I doubt that anyone who played has forgotten it. And out there are thousands of people I have played cricket with and against in hundreds of matches. Maybe we sometimes pass each other in the street without knowing.

There's a strange, connected phenomenon to do with cricket grounds, too. It's an elusive feeling that you sometimes get when passing a ground that you think you once played at. It happened to me a few months ago, for the first time in a couple of years. I was driving through a town somewhere when the road became familiar in a way that might have been real or imagined. On one side was a high wooden fence with another chain-linked one behind it, reaching even higher. Ivy was growing up through its gaps. The traffic slowed, caught by a set of pedestrian lights just ahead. Through a couple of fence panels that had warped and come apart from one another I caught sight of a blade-width of green field and a fragment of a two-storey pavilion, then, in the next gap, a section of scoreboard.

It felt right away like I had played there. I could even recall a fragment of the game, fielding second while their opening bat, a big lad with black hair and a Gray-Nicolls, started belting the bowling indiscriminately over mid-on and midwicket, not slogging exactly but swinging, the ball falling just out of reach of the fielders who, in true club style, were being carefully positioned to stop the delivery just gone. I don't remember much more: he hit quite a few, but got out eventually. They probably won. What really came back was the cast of the ground – its shape, its size — and the weather, which was warm but overcast, the sky full of darkening summer clouds with no wind to move them.

The traffic eased, and the ground was gone. There was an old painted sign with the name of the club on it, but I couldn't quite read it in the rear-view mirror. It probably wouldn't have helped. The feeling was almost dream-like in the way it refused to become clearer or more solid in the memory. It certainly happened, but did it happen there?

I've played a lot of cricket in a lot of places, and lots of it was a long time ago now. Where do they go, those games and those places . . . If I had to sit down with a piece of paper, I'm not sure how many I'd remember. It seems to take something more than just effort to bring them back; it needs a sense memory or a chance encounter that trips some kind of synapse. It's the odd and ethereal familiarity that you have been somewhere before.

Sometimes I dream about playing on unknown grounds, too, so perhaps a place occasionally makes something imaginary seem slightly more real.

It's a strange sensation, and it's not one that needs a definite answer even if that answer existed. These are the ghost grounds of half-remembered games, and sometimes they reappear, the place itself solid and real, the memory less so.

I read somewhere that guitar makers like Fender and Gibson stay afloat not from sales to pro musicians or kids starting bands but to middle-aged men returning to music as a hobby with the cash to buy top-end instruments. It is the same for the makers of cricket bats. On any given match day there are thousands of pounds worth of bats lying around our dressing-room, and in hundreds of others. A bat is all you have as a batsman, and the thought that a new one will bring with it the fulfilment of dreams seems irresistible and the batmakers know it. A bat is a symbol, a totem, invested with hope, subject to the forces of superstition and luck, the single prop for the vulnerable, suggestible psyche of the batsman. For much of the history of the game batmakers were behind the curve. The hints were there – WG wrote to Gray-Nicolls to congratulate them on one of his blades, a sweet longing evident between the lines of his letter – yet the psychology only began to be exploited with the defining bats of the 1970s and early 1980s, Stuart Surridge's ridge-backed Jumbo and Gray-Nicolls' GN100, known universally as the Scoop (got my first hundred with a beloved Scoop, now in my personal bat Valhalla).

Then came the epic reinvention of the object itself – the supercharged, hyper tooled, bigger, deeper, thicker bats of the new century. The marketing has roared ahead with them, into areas in which men buy: sex, technology, power. Batmakers spend as much time over the product names and their livery as they do over the bats themselves, because, like cars and guitars, image is everything ('you can make the best bat in the world,' one batmaker told me sadly, 'but if your stickers are no good, it won't sell . . .'). And those bats are carefully targeted, not at reality but at fantasy, at self-image.

For louche occupants of the top order, those who arrive at the ground in middle-age crisis cars, come bats that sound like 1970s hairspray or pub-machine condoms: the

TP Willow Rumpus, the Samurai Keibo, the Kookaburra Rogue, the Woodstock Curve Platinum, the Vulcan Apollo, the Chase Lancer, the GM Epic DXM, the Willostix Anaconda, the Matrrixx Gladius, the Black Cat Phantom, the Puma Cobalt, the Adidas Libro, the Charlie French Recurve.

There are military-themed willow weapons for weekend warriors who talk loud, work in sales, turn up in two-year-old 4x4s that take up three spaces in the car park, who bat six and think of themselves as 'the finisher': the Newbery B52 Bomber, the Kookaburra Recoil, the Instinct Sniper Upper Class, the Hawk X-Bow, the Gray-Nicolls Quantum Warrior, the Hunts County Reflex Reckless, the Boom Boom Blaze, the Bulldog Spirit, the Choice Willow Teutonic, the Instinct AK47, the Newbery Uzi.

Joining them but with a more gothic hue are bats for the kids pushing for that second-team place, who get dropped off by their dads and moodily reread *We Need To Talk About Kevin* in the pavilion, who want a bat that sounds like an obscure Iron Maiden B-side: the Hell4Leather 666 Monster, the Gray-Nicolls Oblivion Slayer, the Willostix Medusa, the Newbery Mjolnir, the SAF Hades, the Choice Willow Immortal, the Vulcan Fire, the Hunts County Mettle Monster.

For the man who looks upon batting as a higher calling, who sees mysticism in its challenges, who trusts in luck and destiny, who is retraining as a counsellor and arrives in a nine-year-old Volvo on the back of which one of the lads has written 'clean me': the GM Luna, the Choice Willow Saladin, the Vulcan Zeus, the Surridge Ocre, the SF Sapphire, the Solitaire Pink, the SAF Infinity. There

is the totally left field and slightly unintelligible: the Piri
Piri Tampiqueno Dias Pro (although kudos for fitting it
all on the sticker), the Salix Praestantia, the Adidas Pellara.

There is even a prime cut, a slice so rare that it takes the
object beyond function and into form, from artisanship
and into art. Newbery, noble podshavers of Sussex, offer
the Cenkos, a bat that costs a grand, made to the buyer's
specifications. That, though, however beautiful (and it is)
is still a tool. Laver & Wood's Signature range is something
very slightly different. In 13 years, James Laver has found
just 87 pods of willow good enough for the Signature, and
the first of those he kept for himself. The extraordinary
thing about the others is they are supplied with an exact
copy of the bat made from the next grade of willow down,
'if you prefer to keep the Signature as a piece of art'. It
also comes with a display stand. It's strange and wonderful
and slightly sad to think of a bat that might actually be too
beautiful to use, and yet here it is. That James Laver makes
them far away on the edge of the world in New Zealand,
mailing them out once they are finished (and the bounty
of $1,999NZ is handed over) only adds to the mystery of
their creation. Even Laver himself is slightly in awe: 'The
finished bat is always a marvel to behold, and it is often a
shame to let it leave the workshop.'

Bats like that are at the very edge of actually being bats,
unique and beautiful objects that transcend their purpose
to exist simply as art, as examples of what can be done.
They fire the imagination, not the ball.

In Timothy O'Grady's wonderful short book *On Golf*,
he recalls his dad, a fine low-handicapper, attending the

funeral of the father of a fellow player. The service passes
solemnly and the guests file past the casket to offer their
condolences. As O'Grady's dad reaches the end of the line,
his friend asks him gravely for a private word and ushers
them through the other mourners into a private room.
His friend closes the door, assumes his golfing stance and
says helplessly: 'Do you think if I were to move my right
hand a little bit further under the shaft . . .'

The obsessive mindset is not so much to do with golf
or cricket or guitars or any subject in particular, but
in some way pertains to being male. Across Mumbai's
packed maidans, the grizzled realms of grade cricket in
Australia, the courtyards of Pakistan, on Antiguan beaches
and English village greens, on artificial pitches in Japan
and Afghanistan, in Estonia and Canada, New York and
Prague, the same look in the eye of the men playing can
be seen, that curious, glorious kind of tunnel vision of
the devotee. Amateur cricket can be somewhere to retreat
into, to allow such feelings full expression. Many of the
men I play cricket with are high-achievers, distinguished
in their field, yet the mania of self-delusion grips them just
as hard, sometimes harder. Each season we have threats of
retirement, compulsive stockpiling of expensive equipment, disbelief at consistent and predictable failure, and
defiance of one of cricket's immutable laws, 'do what you
always do, get what you always get'.

But at the start of each season, we have a constant
renewal of joy and hope, of the chance to dive back in
and do it all over again.

Badly.

6
Professionals

Each night before he went out to bat for Australia, Ricky Ponting would write a list of what he needed to do at the crease:

- watch the ball
- play straight
- loud calls
- be patient
- be positive in attack and defence
- bat for a long time
- make 100
- be man of the match
- be man of the series.

Having written each point down, he would then underline them one by one while reading the list aloud as he visualised performing each action successfully. He would then write a list of the bowlers he expected to face, and noted how he thought they would try to bowl at him. He would then visualise the deliveries intended to get him out and how he would stop them. Immediately afterwards he would turn off the light and go to sleep.

When the Australian openers walked out, he would sit down with all of his gear laid out around him in exactly the same way each time. He would chew three pieces of gum and sip a bottle of water. When a wicket fell, he'd take out the gum, drink the rest of the water and walk out to bat, for which he had another specific checklist:

- display energy and walk fairly quickly
- do three or four butt kicks with each leg
- play a number of shadow straight drives while walking
- flick wrist with bat in hand – both hands.

Once at the crease, yet more ritual. He took a middle-stump guard from the umpire and then began to 'clear' any real and imagined bits of turf, stud marks, dirt and other 'rubble' until the crease was 'totally clean'. He would then go and look at the point on the pitch where he felt the bowler was going to try and land his first delivery and make sure that was clear too. He would walk to the side of the pitch and touch his toes a couple of times with bat in hand. Then he'd return to the crease, study the field setting and only then prepare to face up.

As the bowler ran in he would say to himself 'watch the ball' at two pre-determined points, the first half-way through the bowler's run, the second as the bowler approached the crease. Just before release he would look at the spot on the wicket where he thought the ball was going to land and then looked back up to watch the bowler deliver.

'Then,' he said, 'whatever happens, happens . . .'

Ponting batted 287 times for Australia in Test matches and another 365 times in one-day internationals. That's 652 evenings of writing that list (more if you include the occasions on which he was not out overnight). He faced 22,782 deliveries in Tests and another 17,046 in one-dayers. That's 39,828 looks down at the wicket and 79,656 exhortations to himself to 'watch the ball'. It worked, all of that work. He scored 13,378 Test runs, more than everyone except Sachin Tendulkar, and 13,704 one-day runs, which is more than everyone except Tendulkar and Kumar Sangakkara. In all he passed a hundred 71 times, which is more than anyone except Tendulkar. He was dismissed for nought 37 times, which is just over 5 per cent of his innings.

When he first left Launceston, Tasmania, to train at the Australian academy in Adelaide, the head coach there, Rodney Marsh, called him, 'the best 16-year-old I've ever seen'. One of the biggest challenges faced by young professional batsmen is working out a method to cope with very quick short-pitched bowling. Marsh's classes were simple: he cranked a bowling machine as fast as it would go and made them duck and weave as balls whistled past their ears. He called it 'bouncer evasion'. He noticed that Ponting seemed to get into position more quickly than the others.

'Try and hit one . . .' he said to Ponting.

Ponting did. And then another, and another. Marsh began asking him to hit one in front of square, the next behind square and so on. Ponting did that, too. Marsh was astonished. The other players had a go. None could connect. Two of them were struck on the head trying.

The pull shot would become the bedrock of Ponting's attacking game against fast bowling. Opponents would usually respond by pitching fuller to him so he developed his dominant drive back down the ground, a deadly double punch that minimised the length on which a bowler had to land the ball. The ability to pull came, he thought, from always being the smallest kid in the team when he was growing up. He instinctively developed a method of coping with what were to him high-bouncing deliveries. His backlift, which came from cocking his wrists, made it easier for him to drop the bat down onto the ball. The rest of it was talent. And although Tim Noakes had demonstrated that the top batsmen didn't necessarily have better eyesight than anyone else, team-mates of Ponting noticed that he would often talk to them about things he had seen happening in the crowd while he was batting out in the middle.

It would be easy to say that Ponting's epic career was preordained. He was right up there in the highest echelon of batsmen to have played the game after all.

And yet, that routine, day after day, month after month, year upon year . . .

I once watched Ponting and Shane Watson, destroyer of Simon Kerrigan, go through their batting drills before a one-day international against England at Southampton. They came down to the boundary edge in front of me with one of the coaches, who began giving Watson some gentle throw-downs. Watson pounded the ball back past him, each one thudding into the advertising hoarding with a heavy thump. He wandered off and Ponting took over. He struck the ball hard, too, but where Watson's drives all went back past the thrower, Ponting hit each shot to a different point on the field simply by controlling the face of the bat with his wrists. It was a small and subtle difference that demonstrated Ponting's attention to detail and the way his mind worked. That game was his 347th one-day appearance.

There is a small part of the amateur game at the top rung of club and grade cricket where the amateur and professional worlds collide. Teams there will employ a professional for a season – usually a young talent – and the amateurs that play will probably have flirted with selection for higher office. But, in general, the gap is vast. Professionals bat, bowl and field better. They make fewer mistakes, and their mistakes are by finer margins. They have a greater range of shot, and they know which one to use and when. They understand risk and when to accept it, and they are in better control of their emotions. They think more clearly under pressure. They know their game more intimately and for much of the time they play within themselves. There is a certainty to their judgement that the amateur lacks, because there are consequences to a lack of judgement that the amateur will never face. Just as a club chess player and a grand master can look at the same board and see two entirely different things, so the professional cricketer perceives the game in a way that the amateur doesn't. They have what Martin Amis called a 'natural severity' in their dealings with the ball. What's more, they look entirely natural and at ease on the field, their world both observable, and yet intimate and closed to outsiders.

I once played in a game with the former England seamer Ed Giddins. He'd been retired for a decade, and hadn't bowled at all that season. He took the new ball. I looked at the wicket after his first over – six deliveries had landed within a foot of each other on a perfect length. The batsman had played and missed at five. I asked Ed how fast he thought he was bowling.

'Seventy-three miles an hour,' he said, with some certainty.

Later he'd talked about how much he'd loved bowling as a kid. He hung a large black tarpaulin in his back garden and bowled into it all day, right through the summer. As a result, his action was so grooved, his muscle memory so ingrained, that he could not play for a year and then come back and immediately put the ball where he wanted, time after time.

I expect that kind of childhood is common to most pros. They have a devotion not just to playing but to practice. As a kid, Sachin Tendulkar would be ferried around Mumbai by car so that he could play three matches in a day, only batting in each. Tendulkar is said to have spoken to his brother and mentor Ajit about every innings he ever played, from childhood until retirement. Kevin Pietersen, decried by many as a maverick who turned it on and off as he felt like it, was regarded as the hardest trainer in the England side. During one bad patch, he flew from England to South Africa for a weekend simply to have a net with his mentor Graham Ford. Shivnarine

Chanderpaul, one of nine men in history to have scored more than 11,000 Test runs, employed his own net bowlers because he liked to practise for six hours at a stretch. Graham Gooch, who scored more runs in professional cricket than anyone else, including Grace and Hobbs, was a fitness fanatic and the man who changed the culture of the England cricket team in the 1990s, sweeping away an era of which Simon Barnes wrote: 'To be accepted, you had to hate the press, hate practice, enjoy a few beers and what have you . . .' Gooch even invented the now ubiquitous 'Dog Thrower' side-arm device that enables non-bowling coaches to fire balls very rapidly at their batsmen. There is probably no man on earth who has spent more of his life in a cricket net.

His former opening partner Geoffrey Boycott was a master of chiding team-mates into greater efforts when he faced them in practice. An England colleague, John Lever, recalled: 'He was an expert at winding up bowlers . . . He'd say anything to stir you up. "Ah, you're not really bowling, Jake [Lever's nickname] . . . You're not coming in very well . . . Are you injured, Jake?" Then in your annoyance you'd come rushing in and suddenly he was having a good net.'

Viv Richards liked to face the entire West Indies pace battery in the nets, safe in the knowledge that nothing out on the field would be as fearsome. Ricky Ponting insisted that all of the Australian fast bowlers use new balls at him in the nets, because that was what he'd face most often in a game situation.

There are exceptions, of course. David Gower batted in lordly fashion for many years and famously loathed

nets, especially the 'naughty boy' variety imposed after
a poor performance (yet he is very interesting on the
necessity for mental renewal – he felt he played better if
he could get away from the game for a while and think
about something else). Naturally fit and strong men like
Fred Trueman and Ian Botham reserved their energy for
the field of play and still did mighty deeds year after year.
Shane Warne felt that coaches 'were for getting you from
the hotel to the ground'. And ultimately the repetition of
practice long into adulthood can grind away at the body
and at the will. In the modern age, the daily drilling of
skills when allied to the number of matches has led to
burnout and mental fatigue.

The other great area of experience that professionals
have and amateurs never will are the days spent in the
field, which can seem endless. Mark Ramprakash, who
loved the game so much he played on until he was 42,
admitted the one thing he didn't miss at all, ever, was fielding. 'Sometimes you just stand there watching the clock
and it barely seems to be moving,' said Andrew Flintoff.
'All you're thinking is, when's lunch . . .'

The longest that I've fielded for in recent years is 47
overs. The professional's day is usually 90. Spare a thought
for the 1938 Australians, who spent 335 overs in the field,
the most ever, as England scored 903-7. Perhaps the
greatest disregard for the discipline came from Pakistan's
languid and joyous batsman Inzamam ul-Haq. At the
crease, his shots flowed like water (although he was well
known as a dreadful runner) and he hated being dismissed: he once took so long to walk off after an lbw
that the game had actually restarted before he crossed the

rope. The former England bowler and *Guardian* cricket correspondent Mike Selvey tells a wonderful story about watching Pakistan practise before a Test in Karachi under the coaching of Javed Miandad. They warmed up strenuously, all of which 'passed Inzy by . . . he was yet to leave the air conditioning of the dressing room. Fielding drills followed, during which he emerged, tracksuited and padded up. He wandered across to a large wicker chair by the nets and slumped down to observe the efforts of his teammates. Then came a net session that he also viewed nonchalantly for a while before deciding it was time for a spot of batting. So he unzipped his top, removed it, placed his green Pakistan helmet on his head, and strolled into the nearest net, where for twenty minutes he proceeded to bat like a prince, before deciding enough was enough. [He] disappeared back to the dressing room, not to be seen again. Next day, of course, he made a century.'

But professionals, too, must inhabit the game's great hinterland of doubt and fear. A career in cricket is in part about the accrual of scar tissue, the thousand and one small cuts of disappointment and defeat that weigh on the psyche and extract their price. What was once all youthful certainty can become a dark adult world in which a living must be made and then maintained against the forces of form and injury and age. The player must then stagger from the wreck of a faded professional career into a world outside of the bubble that the game creates around them. Only recently have these feelings and forces come to be acknowledged and understood. Of a single generation of

England players, Marcus Trescothick retired prematurely from a successful international career with a stress-related illness, and his subsequent book made public the subject for the first time. Graham Thorpe endured a dreadful crisis over the public break-up of his marriage and estrangement from his children. Jonathan Trott retreated with acute stress from England's last Ashes tour and later retired from international cricket after trying bravely to resurrect his career in the West Indies. Steve Harmison suffered throughout his career with a form of homesickness which he later discovered was symptomatic of a deeper depression that lasted for a decade. Depression also affected Andrew Flintoff, who escaped the stresses of the England captaincy by binge-drinking, and Matthew Hoggard, who almost broke down on the field in a Test match against New Zealand. Simon Jones, who with Flintoff, Hoggard and Harmison made up the 'Famous Four' of pace bowlers that slayed the mighty Australians in the indelible Ashes series of 2005, lost the rest of his international career to a succession of serious injuries. He became so desperate to recover that by 2009 all he could think of as he spent Christmas Day – also his birthday – with his wife and young sons was that he couldn't wait for the gym to open the next morning so that he could start training again. When he accepted that he would have to retire, 'the relief was massive. I hadn't realised the stress I was under until it was gone. I didn't have to wake up in the morning consumed by thoughts of my knee or training or pain or money. My body began to feel better almost right away. The scary thought, however, was what do I do now?'

That is a question that every professional must face and then answer. Only in the last decade have a dazzling few earned the sort of money that allows them the freedom to choose whether to work or not. It's not the experience of the majority, even in a game increasingly awash with television money and opportunities for franchise employment. Some – again just a few – slip seamlessly into coaching and a continuation of the lifestyle. Perhaps slightly more, usually the already famous, go into the comm boxes and press galleries and radio studios of the world. But the destinations of others, and what they do there, is disparate, unremarked on, often prosaic (although the quirky Andy Caddick has become a helicopter salesman, which is probably unique). What must also be resolved is a relationship with the game that has defined them. It is gloomy to return to David Frith and his book *Silence of the Heart*, but what led him to explore cricket's suicides was the idea that 'it was the loss of cricket that hurt men, sometimes fatally'. Peter Roebuck told him that he thought cricket 'drew people of a fragile nature in the first place'. Mike Brearley, in his foreword to the most recent edition of *Silence*, added: 'this book forces me to work through an idea that I have long held: that cricket more than any other sport helps a person work through the experience of loss by virtue of forcing its participants to come to terms with symbolic deaths on a daily basis . . . One might have hoped that such a process of emotional learning would be a source of strength to the cricketer, enabling him to mourn, cope with and make the best of the loss of his beloved profession on retirement.'

There is no doubt that a professional cricketer's last day on the field brings a moment of reckoning. They have probably sensed its onset, even if they're not being shoved out of the door by the non-renewal of a contract or an injury that won't heal. Calibrated to judge themselves, they would feel the fine edge of their skills beginning to blunt. Unconscious actions first become conscious and then unperformable. In Ricky Ponting's penultimate Test, against South Africa in Adelaide, he was bowled by Jacques Kallis with a full ball that knocked him off his feet. He ended up, humiliatingly, on his hands and knees with the wicket broken behind him. He was clean bowled in the second innings, too, and knew that the end was upon him. Several batsmen have spoken of the strange sensation of seeing the ball but being unable to react to it, a message both unwanted and undeniable.

Geoffrey Boycott lingered at Scarborough long after his final match as a professional, for Yorkshire against Northants, had ended in a tame draw. 'Something had come to an end, something wonderful,' he said later. 'I just thought, this is it then. I waited for the ground to clear. Then I wandered around on my own, among all the newspapers and food wrappers and tin cans.'

He felt the loss almost like a bereavement. He retired in 1986 aged 46. In 1999, when he was 59, he wrote: 'I miss playing to such an extent that I can honestly say I would exchange the rest of my life for five more years of playing for England at the height of my form.' It was a view that only softened after a nearly fatal onset of throat cancer: 'when you're just jumping in a wooden box and you manage to jump out again, it's quite an experience.' Even so, his wife Rachael said that he could still experience intense emotions when remembering the high points of his career.

Like many ex-pros, Boycott refused to play in veterans' games or benefit matches. Ian Botham is another who hasn't picked up a bat since his retirement. Alec Stewart, Mike Atherton, Nasser Hussain and Graham Thorpe haven't either. Others feel differently. Darren Gough has a team that plays charity games. Lashings field an all-star XI that – for a fee – play all comers. Many more do the same. David English, who runs the Bunbury XI, recalls Barry Richards flying in from Australia for a game against Norma Major's XI at Alconbury: 'He had no gear, just a well-worn pair of golf shoes. With hastily borrowed kit and a bat so old it had cobwebs on it, he stood, bespectacled at the crease. Barry hadn't batted for twelve years but he scored 52 that day.'

Even so, some miss the camaraderie and the safety of the dressing-room too deeply. Brearley felt that jobs 'that make use of a man's name and previous skills' could in time cause a lack of 'authenticity' and sense of self – a piercing description of the celebrity-driven, reality TV age that was looming into view as he wrote. There are some that can take this life of charity dinners and golf club days and tour group holidays as they pose for endless photos and answer the same old questions about the glory years over and over, but some have the thousand-yard stare and listless posture of men living in a dimly lit and rapidly receding past.

Real life intrudes, too. One of cricket's saddest losses was that of David Bairstow, the Yorkshire and England wicketkeeper who took his own life at the age of 46. An apparent extrovert, there were a thousand and one stories about 'Bluey' and his long-running double act with Arnie Sidebottom, Yorkshire's equally redoubtable seamer. As David Hopps, a wonderful writer on cricket who covered the Yorkshire beat during the three years of Bairstow's captaincy, noted, 'he liked to be on first-name terms with the entire crowd, at least those he was still talking to'. Bairstow was proud, combative, hot-headed, 'an indomitable spirit', as Hopps put it, 'and assured of a popularity that ranks alongside anyone in the county's history', and yet it was not enough. When he died, according to his obituary in *Wisden*, he had been suffering from depression. His wife was ill, he had financial troubles, he was facing a charge of drink-driving and he was suffering from the pain of the injuries he'd accrued over a long career. It was, in that terrible moment, overwhelming for him.

Speaking to David Frith for his book, Viv Richards said, 'It is what people do to themselves that causes their turmoil.' Ultimately, cricket can be too much or not enough, and indivisible from real life.

If there is one sentence that the pro hears most often from the amateur, usually after a lacklustre performance or a moan about the number of matches, it's that they 'would do your job for nothing' (to which the pro must be sorely tempted to reply 'well, you'd have to because no one would pay you'). Superficially, from the outside, it is a fantasy life. But the game's finances are baroque and work, broadly, on a trickle-down effect from the international series and tournaments that generate large broadcast contracts which are then in part redistributed to subsidise the first-class teams that produce and nurture new players. These forces have been distorted by shifting power structures and political alliances between nations that would (and have) taken entire books to examine, and they are weighed against cricket's anachronistic nature. A long and rambling game designed for the Victorian age does not fit with modern life, and yet it has barely changed. Much of what the marketing men would call 'product' takes place when its potential audience is at work or otherwise engaged. It's in part why Twenty20 cricket has been revolutionary, and its franchise tournaments have had a role in the creation of the 'freelance cricketer': Chris Gayle, the Grace or Bradman of T20 batting in its formative period, has represented 12 teams, including such luminaries as Matabeleland Tuskers and the Barisal Burners, and created for himself via Twitter an image of globetrotting international playboy, a gun for hire who competes on his own terms. He is divorced from the West Indies national side – for whom he has scored two Test match triple-centuries (Triple Century is also the name of the 'sports bar' he's opened in Jamaica) – in part due to injury but in part because they can't afford to pay him.

Interviewed for Sam Collins' documentary film *Death of a Gentleman** Gayle revealed that he was earning a thousand US dollars for appearing in an ODI for West Indies. Given that he receives a base fee of $650,000 for the six-week

*Declaration of interest – I was one of the co-writers of the film, along with Sam and Jarrod Kimber. Anyone interested in a more detailed and damning telling of the story of N. Srinivasan, Lalit Modi and the creation of the Big Three can find it there.

Indian Premier League season and around $250,000 for Australia's four-week Big Bash tournament, it's probably fair to say that he makes more per minute of batting in franchise cricket than he would playing an ODI series for West Indies. He has often been called a mercenary, but as he says in the film, 'you have to be realistic . . .'.

Gayle may be symptomatic of cricket's future, but he has not created it. The game's apartheid was once empire and then colour. Now it is power. In 2014, under the influence of the cement company magnate N. Srinivasan, India's board of control, the BCCI, exercised the power of its billion-strong audience and joined with the boards of England and Australia to create a new 'Big Three' of countries that would receive and control the bulk of the game's worldwide revenues. It meant that the other seven Test-playing nations, already struggling to pay their big names anything like the sums they could make in franchise cricket and reliant on the Big Three to agree to play lucrative bilateral series with them, ceded almost all power over their future, and the health of the game. West Indies were already riven by disputes between team and board and have been reduced to fielding an international side shorn of its best players, who are sometimes appearing elsewhere in the same country for more money. Afghanistan, where cricket has been a remarkable success and a unifying force, have been excluded from a World Cup. Zimbabwe has seen much of its funding disappear into its weak and corrupt internal structure, and so on.

In the face of such naked commerce, it seems absurd to denigrate cricketers for cashing in where they can, because the profession has always been a fight between employers

and its workforce. Very few players in history have possessed
the box office clout that enables Chris Gayle or Kevin
Pietersen or M. S. Dhoni to control their own destiny.

Cricket's first great modern schism can now be seen
as a futuristic shudder: the Australian media baron Kerry
Packer established World Series Cricket in direct opposition to the existing international game in 1976, in a fight
over television rights that he ultimately won. The 'rebel'
players who took his money, including the then England
captain Tony Greig, who was promised (and got) a job for
life by Packer, were at first traduced and then accepted
and now celebrated. The era is bathed in a Technicolor
seventies nostalgia of tight shirts, hipster flares and macho
moustaches – there is a wonderfully evocative Australian
TV mini-series called *Packer's War*, based on Gideon
Haigh's book, that is a treat for anyone who wants a
primer on the story.

South Africa's exclusion from world sport during the
apartheid years, a boycott led by cricket, was nonetheless
broken by 'rebel' tours, seven in all, and among the players who went were Graham Gooch, Geoffrey Boycott,
Mike Gatting, Kim Hughes, Rodney Hogg and Alan
Knott. For the English and Australian touring teams,
bans and opprobrium were handed out in equal measure, but the divisions were never permanent and grudges
slipped away. Players had their own reasons for going,
often financial but often, too, the opportunity to play a
kind of 'international' cricket that they otherwise did not
have the chance to play. None were so benighted as the
two unofficial West Indies sides that went in 1982–3 and
1983–4. They were brilliant players who, had they been

born at almost any other time in cricket history, would have walked into the national team. They simply had the misfortune to play when even better players stood ahead of them.

Many of the 18 who went never recovered from the life ban handed down to them. The touring party included Sylvester Clarke, probably the most brutally quick bowler in the world and the only man Viv Richards ever admitted to feeling 'uncomfortable' facing, who battled a drink problem and died of a heart attack aged 45; Richard 'Danny Germs' Austin, the 'right-handed Sobers' who died in 2015 after a life of homelessness, begging and drug addiction; Lawrence Rowe, who emigrated to Florida to escape the fallout; Franklyn Stephenson, 'the greatest all-rounder never to play for West Indies', who claims that he still can't find employment as a coach because of the stigma; and David Murray, son of Everton Weekes, who now walks the beaches of Barbados selling 'stuff' to tourists.

As Siddhartha Vaidyanathan wrote of them: 'They left their country as villains and became heroes in another. With hindsight it can now be said they were neither.'

Fear is an unexamined subject in the pro game. As with boxers, it can be fatal even to admit fear to oneself in the mind, let alone say it out loud, but the professional cricketer must confront not just nerves and mental anguish or the fear of failure or decline, but the physical threat of very fast bowling.

The name of Sylvester Clarke is receding now, but during the first half of the 1980s in his years as Surrey's opening bowler it hung over county cricket in the same way that Sonny Liston's had hung over boxing: star-crossed, whispered, feared . . . His first-class figures – 942 wickets at 19.52 – suggest an outstanding talent; his 11 Tests – 42 wickets at 27.85 – hint at a man born out of time. Yet the numbers are like the list of Sonny Liston's knockouts: a simple frame on which to drape the myth.

When Steve Waugh joined Peter Roebuck's Somerset in 1986, he felt the will of his team-mates 'disintegrating' a full week before their appointment with Sylvester. By the time the players were getting changed for the game, he wrote in his autobiography, 'half of them were out already'. When Waugh himself went to the crease he faced 'the most awkward and nastiest spell' of his career. He described the experience as 'something you can't pre-pare for. It's an assault both physically and mentally and the moment you weaken and think about what might happen, you're either out or injured . . .'

Waugh was hardly alone. Graham Gooch had his helmet split down the middle by a Sylvester Special. Zaheer Abbass was struck so hard that his lid had an indentation as deep as half of the ball. David Gower had the padding and thumb guard ripped from his hand, along with most of his thumbnail – they ended up 'near third slip'. Middlesex seamer Simon Hughes, hit on the head by the third ball he ever faced from Clarke, wrote from the blessed safety of retirement that he had been left 'two millimetres of man-made fibre from death'.

Whether he was the quickest of his time is a moot point. What set Sylvester Clarke apart were two things. The first was his attitude at the crease. He was in a way unknowable; wordless, dead-eyed. All that was clear of his personality was the way he bowled – with bad intentions.

Once, challenged by an umpire for repeatedly pitching short, he turned around and said: 'it ain't no ladies' game . . .' The second was that his pace was accompanied by steepling bounce, and, worse than that, an action that made it unpredictable. From a short, slowish run his natural line was towards the batsman. Dennis Amiss, who made that double hundred against Michael Holding and Andy Roberts at the Oval in 1976, called it 'the trapdoor ball', because it was hard to pick up and then it just kept zoning inwards at the throat like a heat-seeking missile. Superficially it seems as though Sylvester might have been a legend (or at least a different kind of legend) had he not been born at a time of astonishing abundance in West Indies fast bowling, but that was not his fate. Like Liston, he appears to have been an outsider. On a rare tour with West Indies to Pakistan, he was pelted with fruit and rubbish by the crowd in Multan. He threw a brick boundary marker back at them and seriously injured a spectator. A couple of years later he went on the tour of South Africa. Then there was the rum. There is a famous story that Clarke was discussing his life with a journalist in Barbados, where he'd returned after his retirement. Pushed on whether his career had been affected by Clive Lloyd's selection policies or the rebel tour, he looked at the bottle on the table and said, 'that ruined my career'.

His *Wisden* obituary retells the tale of his day as a net bowler when England toured West Indies in 1993, long after he'd packed up professionally. He arrived at the

Bridgetown nets wearing plimsolls and no socks, evidently 'well-fortified' on the demon rum and bowled a spell to Graham Thorpe off a short run that was as quick as anything England faced on the tour.

Geoffrey Boycott, who faced them all, thought that Australia's Jeff Thomson and West Indies' Michael Holding at their peak were the fastest. Ricky Ponting said the quickest spell he ever faced came from Shoaib Akhtar in Perth. Graham Gooch felt that West Indies' Patrick Patterson troubled him most. Ultimately, the perception of pace on any given day depends on so many variables of heat, light, form, biorhythms and reaction that an empirical judgement is impossible. The truth is, it's all fast.

In terms of pure pace (as opposed to skill and know-how), quick bowlers peak young. Simon Jones reckoned that he was at his fastest before he turned 20. At the practice day before he won his first Test cap against India at Lord's in 2002 he bowled a ball that nearly hit a young wicketkeeper who was standing 30 yards back. One of the coaches, Bob Cottam, later told him it was the fastest delivery he'd ever seen. Jones admitted he 'wanted to be feared'. 'It's a feeling like no other to know that the opposition are worried about you, sometimes frightened physically and psychologically. I've had guys throwing up in the dressing room toilets before facing me . . .'

Jeff Thomson bowled what the hundred or so people who saw it thought was the quickest spell ever in a Sydney Grade game between Mosman and Bankstown on New Year's Eve 1973, when he was 23 years old. It was brilliantly recreated by Christian Ryan from a series of interviews, a day that began as any other and ended with experienced players like the Bankstown skipper Barry Knight, who played 29 times for England, thinking they'd been present for something otherworldly.

Bankstown's opener Rob Jeffery is hit on the shoulder and collapses on his wicket. Some minutes later, when he goes to take off his pads, he finds that he is shaking. His opening partner John Pym realises what is happening and decides to play almost without a backlift, only to find his leg stump detonated from the ground before he can move his bat a few inches. 'Oh well,' he thinks, 'at least I'm alive.' The next ball clean bowls Billy King. The hat-trick ball hits a dent in the pitch and rears shoulder-high.

By now, the wicketkeeper and slips are nearer to the sightscreen than the stumps. A couple of overs later, one ball leaps over the gloves of Greg Bush and hits him in the face, leaving his eye 'sort of hanging, not sitting cor-rectly in its socket'. David Colley takes guard in his mate's blood. Thomson doesn't like Colley because he's been selected ahead of him for the state side. To wind Thomson up, Colley wears his New South Wales sweater. He's bowled by a ball that not only he cannot hit, but he can-not see. Barry Knight goes in and has a feeling that he has had only once before, when facing Frank Tyson: that of a ball coming so quickly the eye can discern it only as a blur.

Soon it was over. Thomson had figures of six for four. Greg Bush was operated on for a fractured eye socket and spent a month in hospital lying completely still to save his sight. He recovered and returned to cricket.

Thomson was at his most fearsome for another couple of years, until, as Ryan reported, his flatmate was hit in the chest by an innocuous looking medium-pacer and died from a blood clot, leading Thomson to moderate his approach to hitting batsmen, and then 12 months or so later, he suffered a serious shoulder injury which, although he recovered to play again, negated some of his dramatic bounce.

Many years later, I was at Wormsley, the ground built by John Paul Getty on his estate in the Chilterns, for a cricket day. It was an Ashes year, and Thommo was there. He was the kind of pro who loved his afterlife of speaking gigs and personal appearances, and he was feted and fawned over wherever he went. Even more so than Sylvester Clarke's, his playing days had been mythologised by terror. He loved that, too. By the time he got up to speak, he'd had a few beers, and his eyes glinted with mirth. He was wearing the Hooray uniform of red jeans and a blue blazer; set upon his broad shoulders and pipe-cleaner legs it made him look like the kind of guy who joins a soap opera and makes off with the unsuspecting widow's money.

Next to him was the former England batsman David Steele, the bank clerk who went to war, still grey-haired and bespectacled as I remembered him from The Oval in 1976. They fell quickly into type. Thommo stood with one hand in the pocket of his red jeans looking out across the room, while Steele fumbled with the microphone as he told gentle anecdotes about getting lost in the Lord's Pavilion, and being paid in lamb chops for every run he scored by a local butcher. Thommo by contrast told a single story which was about the dismissal of Keith Fletcher at Sydney in 1975.

'I haven't done this one for a while,' he said, almost to himself. 'Me and Dennis [Lillee] had a plan,' he began, 'which was to kill the pricks.' He giggled at this, and we all laughed.

'A couple of them had already gone to the hospital,' he went on, 'a wicket goes down and out comes this little prick Fletcher ['prick', it quickly became apparent, was a term of some endearment to Thommo, and he used it gently, almost with fondness].

'Now, the Pavilion at Sydney is at square leg and Dennis is fielding at third man. I'm at the end of my run and I'm ready to kill the prick you know. But Dennis comes running over from third man all the way to square leg and starts abusing Fletcher. I'm getting mad with Dennis because I'm ready you know. I'm warm and it's coming out well . . .'

'Then Dennis comes running over to me. I'm like: "Yeah Dennis, I know the plan. Kill him . . ."'

'"Yeah," says Dennis. "But I *really* want you to kill this little prick . . ." Then he ran back down to third man.

'Anyway, first ball, too high. Next ball, adjust the radar . . . bang . . . hits him right in the middle of the forehead. Absolutely smack in the middle. I go down to have a look at him and he's got the most perfect six stitch-marks . . .'

Thommo pointed to the spot on his own forehead, and paused for a second, a faraway look in his eyes. He was transporting himself. 'The physio comes on, Bernie Thomas he was called. Fletcher's staggering all over the place, he can't see straight. Someone says, "He'll have to go off . . ." and Bernie says, "he can't, we've already got two in the hospital . . ." So Bernie pushes him back to the crease . . .'

He mimed Bernie Thomas positioning Fletcher into his stance. By now, Thommo was wiping tears of laughter from his eyes. Everyone in the tent was enjoying the story, and, more than that, we were enjoying Thommo's enjoyment of it. He paused.

'So I go back . . .' He wiped his eyes again. 'I go back and you know next ball, BLAM, stumps all over the place. "Off you go you little prick . . ." I'm saying, and then, here comes Dennis, all the way back up from third man, just to abuse him again as he goes off . . .'

By now, Thommo was rocking back on his heels and dabbing at his eyes. 'Ah bloody hell . . .' he said. 'That's what happened, straight up. I haven't told that one for a while, I really haven't.'

Thommo represented something that day, as old professionals do, a game now gone but left sweet in the memory. Had the incident with Fletcher just happened on the ground right in front of us, it would have been impossible to describe it as he had done. It was only funny now, all of this time later, when the blood and the battle had receded.

I wanted to find out how true Thommo's story was, so I looked up the game. It was Test match number 751, Australia versus England at the SCG, fourth Test. Australia won by 175 runs.

Wisden reported: 'On the last day the demoralising effect of Thomson and Lillee was never more apparent. From 68 for no wicket in the 16th over, the score became 74 for three in the 22nd with Edrich on his way to hospital after being hit below the rib-cage first ball by a Lillee skidder . . . Only Amiss, caught off his gloves off a bouncer that cut back, and Fletcher, shaken by a deflection on to his forehead two balls before his dismissal by Thomson, were exempt from blame.'

Fletcher had made 11, and rather than being bowled next ball, he'd been caught by Ian Redpath a delivery later. Maybe Thommo had forgotten that detail, and maybe he hadn't. He knew the story, though, and he knew how he should tell it: as it was in his head rather than as it exists in the record books. Thommo existed in both places, as cricketer and as myth. It was not a bad way for an old pro to live.

7

The Descendants

He could feel it when it happened. He'd score thirty or forty runs and then the field would go back, a sweeper placed on each boundary, and the intensity from the bowler and the other players would drop and he knew that they'd given up. They couldn't get him out and they knew it. He knew he wouldn't get out, too. And they knew that he knew. Not here. Not today. Not any more.

Instead, they just wanted to get him off strike, to limit the damage and get it over with. This was how dominant he had become, in the game that had often seemed like an internal, private war, a game in which some would always consider him a failure.

For season after season, in shadow and in sun, on quiet grounds and on weekday afternoons, he offered up the splendour of his second act, an act of redemption and an act of revenge, one of the towering feats of English batsmanship.

It was May 2013. I was sitting at the top of the Pavilion at Lord's with Mark Ramprakash. Out on the field, Middlesex were facing Derbyshire. It was the kind of day that made you wonder why we played cricket in England, an afternoon of unyielding grey skies and jagged winds, so cold it was hard to see. Far below us the players hunched in their sweaters, their shouts and exhortations to one another bouncing off the empty stands. Even Lord's found it hard to be beautiful, the rows of off-white plastic seats stained and scuffed, the grandstand exposed and showing its age. I was wearing a suit and tie, which was required to get into the Pavilion, but Ramprakash was swathed in a club hoodie and track pants. He had retired from cricket at the end of the previous season and now he was the batting coach at Middlesex. He was also a hero of mine, a batsman to have joined the pantheon of Barry Richards, Geoffrey Boycott and King Viv – although not in the same way, of course. I'd found that my heroes had transmuted from simply being people that I wanted to play cricket with to people that I wanted to write about. And hero was probably the wrong word, although I often used it. I admired his batting but Ramprakash provoked deeper intrigue in me. Maybe I thought that if I could understand something about him and his career, I could unravel something about my own relationship with the game.

As with Barry Richards, the actual connection between Ramprakash and me was tenuous and gossamer-thin. He had been a genuine prodigy, a glimmer of hope for an England team that badly needed one. When he was 18 years old he was man of the match in the Nat West Trophy final playing for Middlesex against Worcestershire. He had a matinee idol smile and an immaculate technique at the crease. But he wasn't just technically correct, he was aesthetically awesome, a throwback to the days when princes

batted like gods for fun. When Ramprakash played a shot –
a cover drive, his rasping back-cut - there was something
aspirational about watching him do it, as if he was embod-
ying the point of the game. He was a descendant of Silver
Billy, 'a sight that would have delighted an artist'. He was
also going to be the saviour of English cricket.

A generational change had arrived with him. Cricket in
the 1980s had been Technicolor, widescreen fun. Tours
were laddish lollapaloozas of booze, birds and big hair.
England's greatest star, Ian Botham, ushered the decade
in with the 1981 Ashes, an unlikely, dramatic and unforgettable win inspired by a man delivering a two-fingered
salute to the frigid and uptight establishment that had just
sacked him as captain. Mustachioed for much of the next
ten years, many of those accompanied by a giant frosted
mullet hairdo, Botham was intergalactically brilliant as a
cricketer and equally talented at getting into strife the
minute he'd walked from the field of play. When he found
a dubious new manager who dressed him in a striped
blazer and a boater and announced that Botham was off to
Hollywood to become 'the next James Bond', it seemed
almost plausible. When he published, with Dennis Coath,
a Tom Sharpe-style cricketing farce called *Deep Cover*
('all-rounder Kevin Sowerbutts is a practical joker with
a taste for the booze and an eye for the birds') it seemed
sure to be a bestseller. When he walked to the crease during a tour game so hungover he forgot his bat, he induced
laughter rather than tut-tutting. When he deliberately ran
out his captain Geoffrey Boycott during a Test match in
New Zealand (the great man allegedly crying 'what have

you done, what have you done?' as Botham sprinted past him to the non-striker's end; Botham's reply, apocryphally, 'I've run you out, you cunt . . .') he carried the rest of the team with him. When he somehow dragged England to the World Cup final in 1992 with a body so broken he could barely bowl medium-pace, it felt like he could summon miracles by sheer force of will. And when he retired in the middle of the 1993 season after a game for Durham against the touring Australians, he paused at the top of his run before his final delivery, unbuttoned his fly and ran in with 'the old man dangling free' as his last farewell.

He was a genuine hero, flawed and imperfect, England's greatest cricketer since Grace. Around him had been other great men: his new-ball partner Bob Willis; the impossibly dashing left-hander David Gower; Botham's spiritual sidekick Allan Lamb; the indomitable Boycott still batting obsessively into his forties; Graham Gooch, a run-making machine; Mike Gatting, a man of appetite for runs, battle and food; John Emburey, parsimonious tweaker and legendary swearer, and his spin-twin, the lordly, disdainful Philippe Edmonds . . . They were like the Wild Bunch, the Dirty Dozen, outgunned by the West Indies side that they could never beat, outlawed by an establishment that still retained the air of the haughty amateur administrator handed power by status.

Botham, Gower and Gatting were all either sacked or resigned their captaincies. In the summer of 1988, the team was skippered successively by Mike Gatting, John Emburey, Chris Cowdrey and Graham Gooch. The most extraordinary appointment was that of Cowdrey, who knew the head of selectors Peter May as 'Uncle Peter'. He got injured during a heavy defeat and was never picked again. Against West Indies and Sri Lanka, May and his panel used 28 players. The following year, they used 29 while losing the Ashes 4-0 to a team described before the series as 'the worst ever to leave Australia'.

Amid this chaos was probably the first generation of players to have become vaguely rich by playing cricket. Yet they were still dependent on the largesse of selectors for their living, paid by the match or by the tour, rushing down motorways to appear for their counties when surplus to England's requirements. Botham and Gower missed a tour of Pakistan because Botham chose to play Sheffield Shield cricket for Queensland, while Gower, with typical elan, went on 'a trip to Africa, a skiing holiday in Europe and a visit to the Winter Olympics in Calgary'.

Unfortunately for them, the entente cordiale that had existed between the touring cricketers and the accompanying journalists was eroded by the rise of red-top culture. Once Ian Botham became a national hero, news reporters joined the cricket beat. Mike Gatting lost his captaincy after an alleged 'romp' with a barmaid, a trumped-up charge that offered cover for the real reason, his on-field spat with the umpire Shakoor Rana in Faisalabad the previous winter;* Botham was busted by a kiss-and-tell from a former Miss Barbados, a highly embellished tale

---

*Rana had initially angered Gatting by wearing a Pakistan jumper while umpiring. Rana then accused Gatting of attempting to move the field while Eddie Hemmings ran in to bowl, an incident which led to the infamous finger-wagging row that was picked up by the stump microphones. Gatting lost almost three years of his England career in the fallout, and the affair led to the introduction of neutral umpires immediately afterwards.

that involved a broken bed. Beefy had, by that time, also admitted to smoking pot in his own newspaper column and was briefly banned from playing. The public life of a cricketer would never again be the same.

With all of its excesses, the 1980s was Test match cricket's rock 'n' roll decade. The players filled grounds and indulged in epic battles before partying like the stars (sometimes literally – Elton John was a semi-permanent fixture on the 1986–7 Ashes tour). A lion on the field, Botham was sometimes deployed as a secret weapon off it, too: on one occasion playing for Somerset against Surrey he disarmed Sylvester Clarke by drinking treble brandies with him in the booze tent at Weston-super-Mare, the subsequent hangover confining Clarke to the dressing-room for the Somerset innings.

As these giants faded, the game they had known went with them. The 1990s were, for English cricket, a time of austerity. The players who came to represent it became worn down by the effort. If the generation of Botham and Gower and Boycott was the generation that I aspired to play with, the next, of Mark Ramprakash, Mike Atherton, Darren Gough, Nasser Hussain, Graeme Hick and Graham Thorpe, was my generation, the players I would have been playing with had I been any good. It was impossible to look at them in the same way because there was less distance between us. They may have done – and sometimes did do – heroic things, but they were not destined to be heroes in the way that Gower and Botham and Willis and Boycott had been, slipping from the small world of cricket into the language of the wider culture. The game for them settled into a lo-fi universe that seemed austere compared to the cinematic excess of the 1980s. Cricket became an attritional thing.

England's position as the game's autocratic, empirical governor slipped away, too. It was clear that the most symbolic matches of the 1980s came in 1984, when the West Indies 'blackwashed' England in a five Test series, the full, crushing realisation of Clive Lloyd's vision for his team. It was a morality lesson, an indication that history was being buried. And the most significant single game of the decade had also been played on English soil, the World Cup final of 1983 at Lord's between West Indies and India, a match I watched from the Tavern with my dad, perfectly placed to see Kapil's famous running catch of Viv Richards. India's upset win did two things: the first was to finally rid India of its sense of cricketing inferiority – it was hard to feel inferior with the World Cup on the sideboard. The second was to ignite a love of limited-overs cricket in the most fervent cricket nation on earth. It was the spark that drove the engine that would power India to the financial and sporting centre of the game.

England, in the nineties, were spear-carriers. In the spotlight centre stage was the duel between West Indies and Australia, the former coming down from their peak, the latter rising toward theirs. When Australia toured the Caribbean in 1995, they faced a team that had not lost a Test series for 15 years. The precise moment of change seemed to come on a terrifying wicket in Trinidad. Steve Waugh swore at, and then faced down, Curtly Ambrose while batting in Australia's first innings and Ambrose had to be pulled away from a physical confrontation. Australia lost the match but won the series and Justin Langer said of Waugh: 'To stand up to the best fast bowler of our time and go toe to toe . . . it gave us a huge boost.'

Soon Waugh was marshalling a team that was even more dominant than those captained by Clive Lloyd and Viv Richards, a team that England were never going to beat. By 1986–7, England had defeated Australia in 86 Tests, Australia had won 87 and 74 had been drawn. When England next won a series in 2005, the score stood at Australia 115 wins, England 93, with 82 draws.

Into this hole fell entire careers; fell the men of my generation. On the field, the game's eternal battle between bat and ball was running the way of the ball. Every bowling record was about to be shattered. Richard Hadlee, who played his final Test match in 1990, had been the first man past 400 Test wickets. By the time the next generation was done, the record would stand at 800. In one-day cricket the top 21 wicket-takers of all time began their careers in or after the 1990s, with the exception of the two pioneers of fast bowling in the era, Wasim Akram and Waqar Younis. Wasim debuted in 1984, Waqar in 1989, and their spiky rivalry and thrilling mastery of the form put them at the point of the arrow. Joining them would be an unprecedented arsenal for the batsmen of the world to contend with: Australia found Glenn McGrath, Shane Warne, Jason Gillespie, Damien Fleming and Brett Lee to join Craig McDermott and Merv Hughes. West Indies' decline was held at bay by the immortal and deadly partnership of Courtney Walsh and Curtly Ambrose, plus Ian Bishop and Patrick Patterson. South Africa, readmitted to international cricket in 1991, produced Alan Donald,

Shaun Pollock and Jacques Kallis, who between them took more than a thousand Test wickets. Sri Lanka, who won the World Cup in 1996 – thus adding their name to a list still missing England's – found the prodigious and controversial Muttiah Muralitharan, and Chaminda Vaas. India's grand old skipper Kapil Dev beat Hadlee's record in 1994, and they discovered their champion leggie Anil Kumble, and Harbhajan Singh. Pakistan had Wasim and Waqar to bowl reverse swing and Saqlain Mushtaq, the inventor of mystery spin.

Those two new and lethal techniques were honed, and the lost art of leg-spin was revived and redefined. Everywhere England's new generation turned, bowling greatness awaited them. Of their major batsmen, only Graham Thorpe would retire with a Test average of more than 40. Mike Atherton, who had the misfortune of opening the batting in this age of fear and nightmares, was dismissed 19 times by Glenn McGrath, 17 by Curtly Ambrose, 17 by Courtney Walsh and ten times by Shane Warne. Almost a tenth of his 212 innings were ducks and his average of 37.69 is the lowest of anyone to score more than six thousand Test runs. And yet he was a giant, the rock of England's batting. Only three players would make more Test runs than Atherton in the 1990s.

If professional sportsmen divide roughly into those with a lust to win and those who simply hate losing – and there is a difference – Atherton certainly belonged to the latter. At times he was like the heroic civil war general under siege from all sides. He resisted South Africa for 643 minutes in Johannesburg in 1995 in his most famous innings, a score of 185 not out that was a citadel of defiance. Against the same opponents at Trent Bridge in 1998 he gloved a ball from Alan Donald to the wicketkeeper Mark Boucher and was given not out as England pursued a target of 247 for victory. Atherton inside-edged his next ball for four, compounding in Donald a pure stream of fury that presented itself as one of the quickest and most aggressive spells of fast bowling seen in England. As the shells flew around him, Atherton hunkered down and rode it out. England won the next morning with him still in situ, his score on 98. Somehow just missing a century seemed to encapsulate his career, a man destined never quite to get the cherry on the top of his cake.

He'd been the kid who had everything, a golden child who was not only an obviously brilliant cricketer from an early age – voted the outstanding schoolboy in the country at 15, captain of the England Under-19 team at 16 – he was academically gifted, too, reading history at Downing College while playing for Cambridge, Combined Universities and Lancashire in the same season. His future seemed gilded and preordained. Even his nickname was 'FEC', which stood for 'Future England Captain' (although it was rapidly repurposed by the Lancashire dressing room, with the usual pro disdain for anyone who has read anything beyond sports autobiographies, as 'Fucking Educated Cunt').

He was England captain at 25, taking over from Graham Gooch for the fifth Test of an Ashes series already lost, then leading the team to the West Indies, where they lost, and then came home for series against New Zealand and South Africa, which were drawn, but during the latter, when the teams met at Lord's, he was accused of ball tampering and lying to the match referee. Raymond Illingworth fined him £2,000 on behalf of the England management and announced the fact sitting next to Atherton at a press conference that was, without anyone's knowledge, broadcast live on television. Atherton's 'crime' was to have transferred dirt onto the ball, an act that arguably wasn't against the Laws at all, and then giving slightly differing versions of events to Illingworth and the match referee, Peter Burge.

Atherton sought sanctuary at a hotel in the Lake District where he was shopped to the press and had to escape to a team-mate's flat. He made 99 in the next match, which he dedicated to 'the gutter press', and was fined for dissent by a vengeful Burge in the final Test of the summer after shaking his head at a terrible lbw decision that saw him dismissed first ball. His first full home summer ended with him climbing over the rooftops of central London on his way out of a dinner party, again desperate to avoid the press. The winter was yet another Ashes tour – and defeat.

And so it went on. Atherton was always outnumbered, always outgunned. He became flint-eyed and inscrutable, closed off to everyone but his team. The personal cost seemed high. What no one knew was that he was struggling with a debilitating and incurable skeletal condition called ankylosing spondylitis which made the constant crouching in his batting stance painful.

Off the field England were caught midway between the autocratic, old-school administration of the 1980s and the fully-integrated, micro-managed structures of today. They appointed a full-time coach for the first time in 1996 (it

was David Lloyd, and when he introduced a fitness con-
sultant and a media relations officer eyebrows could not
have been raised any higher had he announced he was
appointing a psychic and a philosopher to the back-room
team). Central contracts for England players were introduced in 2000, two years after Atherton resigned the captaincy and a year before he retired.

It was a kind of madness that swallowed careers, swallowed men. Atherton would write, years later, that he
'no longer recognised' the person he became while playing through those times. His lieutenant and opening
partner, Alec Stewart, who scored more Test runs than
anyone else in the 1990s, was as relentlessly upbeat as
Atherton was down. Like Ken Barrington, he seemed
to walk out to bat trailing the union flag behind him.
He struck the ball with the timing of a watchmaker, and
once made a hundred in each innings in Barbados, the
fortress of West Indian cricket. Yet with no all-rounder
to replace the irreplaceable Botham, Stewart probably
sacrificed the edge of his batting in turning himself into
a wicketkeeper, too (for a long time he alternated with
one of the game's great eccentrics and the last of the
specialist glovemen, Jack Russell). Stewart and Atherton
were the classic combination of roundhead and cavalier,
and although Stewart was more fun to watch, especially
when he took on fast bowling, it was Atherton I willed
along. His batting was mainly dogged, technically correct but not expansive. He loved to play the hook shot,
though, and I in turn loved him for it. It was as if that
stroke was the little deal he'd done with himself for all
of that denial; a seam of silver in the rock. It was not the

sort of shot you'd imagine he'd play but he played it in the classic fashion, swiping the ball almost off his nose. Of course it's obvious now that he had no choice but to play it — batsmen with bad backs can't duck — but it seemed like the one moment that he allowed the player he wanted to be to show through.

Graham Thorpe and Nasser Hussain became the other stalwarts. It was a shock to watch Thorpe stomp out for his Test debut in the 1993 Ashes. The last time I'd seen him he'd been a tiny little kid on the outfield at Wrecclesham. Now he was broad and stocky, with thick forearms that he used for a whiplash cut shot and, like most lefties, tremendous power off his legs. He got out cheaply to Merv Hughes in his first innings but got a hundred in the second, and his trademark became his ability to come in and counter-attack, even when a couple of early wickets had gone down and the ball was still new. I remembered his brothers Ian and Alan as being exactly the same when we played together, maximising everything they had, never backing down.

Hussain, by contrast, was a raw nerve. In junior cricket he'd been a leg-spinner who batted a bit but he grew, he reckoned, 'a foot' in a single winter and all of a sudden he wasn't just bowling badly but catastrophically, delivering 'triple-bouncers to deadly silence'. He began to work even harder on his batting, the spectre of his father's ambition driving him on, and although he fell behind Atherton, Thorpe and Ramprakash for a while, he debuted in the Test side in 1990 in West Indies. He played twice and was then not selected for another three years. He had an odd way of leaning back when he drove the ball, and all of his intensity and insecurity and ambition roiled inside him, the lava in the volcano.

Every player reacts differently to dismissal. In some it induces a kind of placid contemplation. Most are susceptible to the occasional tantrum. Mike Gatting needed stitches in his hand after punching through the Lord's dressing-room door. The phlegmatic Atherton fractured his big toe kicking a set of scales in Port Elizabeth and once destroyed a bath in the dressing-room at Derby. Even Peter Roebuck was once so angry that he got out of a Somerset team-mate's car and began walking from Hove back to Taunton. Nasser Hussain's ability to clear a dressing-room as he departed the field was second to none. To compound all of his other frustrations he had the unlucky knack of being on the wrong end of some terrible umpiring decisions in a pre-DRS age. He smashed up a fridge in Rawalpindi after being given out lbw to Wasim Akram and broke a crutch belonging to fast bowler Alex Tudor when he copped a poor caught-behind decision from Shane Warne. In Trinidad he was struck plumb in front of the stumps by a ball from off-spinner Carl Hooper that kept so low it almost bounced twice. Hussain stalked straight from the field and into the dressing-room where he punched through a locker with wooden slats and then couldn't get his hand out.*

Mark Ramprakash and Graeme Hick, the other great hope of English batsmanship, arrived into all of this at

---

*When Hussain assumed the captaincy of England in 1999, his bad luck extended to the toss. At one point he lost 14 in a row – odds of 16,384-1.

the same moment, 6 June 1991 at Headingley, the first match of a five-Test series against West Indies. That the two should debut in the same game was a cosmic fluke. Hick, who was born in Zimbabwe, had served a seven-year qualification period before he became available for selection, and he brought with him the apparent certainty of greatness. He was physically imposing, square-shouldered and iron-jawed and he hit the ball murderously hard. Astonishingly, he had already scored 57 first-class centuries, including a famous 405 not out for Worcestershire against Somerset in May 1987, an innings that made the BBC's nine o'clock news. 'Here is a man who could become the most prolific batsman since the great Don Bradman,' wrote Christopher Martin-Jenkins in the *Daily Telegraph*. Ian Botham said, 'Graeme is the best white batsman I've seen . . .'.

Hick was 25 years old, Ramprakash just 22. Hick would bat at three, Ramprakash at five. Headingley, chill and damp in early June, was no place for batsmen, no place for debutants. Even the great Viv Richards, on winning the toss, glanced upwards at the scudding clouds and quickly put England in. His four bowlers were Curtly Ambrose, Courtney Walsh, Patrick Patterson and Malcolm Marshall. Hick was in after 22 minutes when Atherton was castled by Patterson. Ramprakash passed him on the way out 51 minutes later when he'd edged Walsh to Dujon for six. Ramprakash made 27, which with fearful symmetry, was the score he'd make in the second innings, too. It would also, just over a decade later, prove to be his final average.

At the top of the Lord's Pavilion, I asked him what that first day was like.

'I remember facing Ambrose and Walsh early on and I was thinking: "I just don't know how I'm going to score a run here . . ." I wasn't used to that. The bowling was so tight, they gave you nothing. The fielding was brilliant. It was very, very difficult.'

The game became known for an innings often cited as the best ever played by an England batsman, Graham Gooch's 154 not out in England's second dig, when he became the first Englishman to carry his bat since Geoffrey Boycott a decade earlier.

In the rest of the series, Ramprakash made scores of 24, 13, 21, 29, 25, 25 and 19, and then a duck in the one-off Test against Sri Lanka that concluded the summer. Hick followed his first innings 6 with 6, 0, 43, 0, 19 and 1 before he was dropped for the final match. He was selected for the winter tour of New Zealand, but Ramprakash wasn't. The Test match careers of England's great hopes had begun.

It took Mark Ramprakash more than six years and 38 innings to make his maiden Test century, against West Indies in Barbados, an innings that the year's *Wisden* called 'emotional and redemptive'. And yet it could only have been truly redemptive had it not been another 42 innings and three and a half years before his second, and last, in a heavy defeat to Australia at The Oval.

Seven months after that, it was over. On 3 April 2002 at Eden Park, Auckland, Ramprakash played his ninety-second and as it turned out final Test innings. He was bowled by Daryl Tuffey for two. New Zealand won the game and squared a three-match series.

He was 32 years old, and he'd been playing for a decade. His 92 innings can be divided roughly into thirds. Of
his first 30, 20 were against West Indies and four against
Australia. Of his next 36, 13 came against South Africa,
12 against Australia and six against West Indies. Only in
the final third of his Test career, with 14 innings against
New Zealand, a couple versus Zimbabwe and six against
India, did this reign of terror abate, but even then the key
matches were against the 2001 Australians, eight innings
in which he scored 318 runs at 39.75 and made his second
and last Test hundred, 133 at The Oval in an innings defeat.

As the rain came down one afternoon last year, that
hundred was repeated on TV. Contextualised by time
and by the greatness that his opponents would go on to
achieve, it appeared even better now than it was when he
played it.

Graeme Hick, his inverse image, his enigmatic twin,
was done before he was. Hick played the last of his 65 Tests
in March 2001. He had been dropped and reselected 11
times and averaged 31 to Ramprakash's 27. Hick scored six
Test centuries, but none were as famous – or infamous –
as the one he didn't make, at the Sydney Cricket Ground
on England's demoralising Ashes tour of 1994–5. In the
rare position of being able to declare, Atherton called the
England innings off with Hick on 98. For whatever reason, Hick was dithering at the crease and had not tried
to score from the final three deliveries he'd faced. It was a
moment that seemed to summarise the tour and the team
and the times, its captain trying to match the ruthlessness of the teams that were defeating them, the players
unsure how to react to it. The dressing-room went quiet.

Atherton's decision divided opinion. It was impossible to know whether he would have declared on any other batsman. He would say some years later that he felt with hindsight it was a mistake. Hick forgave him quite quickly but didn't speak to the tour manager, Keith Fletcher, for a month. Things drifted on.

Hick hated fuss, that much was clear from the uncomplicated way he batted, but, unusually for a big player, he hated the attention, too. Somewhere in his psyche was not the small, icy chip of selfishness and self-regard that the great men had but something more inhibiting – a lack of confidence. It seemed impossible. How could someone who had essentially never failed suddenly feel that he could not succeed? Nothing, not scoring his first century at the age of six, or making 405 not out as a 21-year-old, or having 56 first-class centuries in the book before playing Test cricket, could overcome it. 'I would be standing at slip watching some other player batting wonderfully and I'd think to myself, "I can't do that" . . .' he said. He found the England dressing-room 'a strange environment'. He'd sit alone in the corner, avoiding the cliques. The three years that Ray Illingworth was the head of selectors were the worst. Illingworth didn't appear to like him. He kept dropping him and was unforgiving of what he saw as Hick's passivity. At Trent Bridge a few months after the declaration debacle in Sydney, Illingworth told him to his face that he thought he was soft. The next day he made a hundred. He admitted to crying when Atherton told him of one of his deselections. Atherton liked him but felt that 'problems tend to remain deep inside and confrontation is rare'. He was complex, shy, diffident, a man who would have understood James Southerton's 'retired thinking he was out'.

As For Ramprakash . . .

In the early days at Middlesex they called him the Bloodaxe. It wasn't temper as such, but an overwhelming intensity, a desire so manifest that it got in his way, became utterly counterproductive. Symmetry had bookended his Test career. But something had changed by the end. In 1998, on tour in the West Indies, he met Steve Bull, a psychologist who was travelling with the team. He told Bull how confident he'd been when he was younger, and how that confidence ebbed the longer he went without a big score in Test cricket. Then he was dropped and recalled, dropped and recalled and he got very nervous, never knowing which chance would be his last, and appearing in Test matches became an unpleasant experience. After speaking with Bull, his results improved significantly, but when he had a little dip in New Zealand in 2002 the Sky commentary team started saying a few things about him on air, and he felt that the knives were out. They got home in early April and the county season, which would be his second for Surrey after switching from Middlesex, started almost right away. He was unbeaten on 70 overnight in a game against Lancashire when the new England coach, Duncan Fletcher, came to see him. Duncan asked a couple of questions about why he hadn't done well, but he didn't really say a great deal in return, didn't offer any thoughts as to how he could improve. Instead they left him out of the Test team, this time forever . . .

Surrey were a good side, fighting for promotion, so he threw himself into it. The Bloodaxe was still there – for a while he was enraged by the new car parking charges at the Tube station near his house, so he began cycling to The Oval with his gear on his back, ridiculous really when he had to do the same again at the end of a long day's play. When he started driving again his team-mates would joke that if he scored runs they'd hear soul music on the stereo and he'd be smiling at people and waving them out into the road in front of him, but, if he'd failed, it would be hip hop at top volume and back to the rat race. But he was a different player, more reflective, more accepting, calmer, better . . .

The county used to produce a handbook at the start of each season and one year he looked in it and saw that he'd made 80 first-class centuries, and it occurred to him that, if he stayed fit and retained his form and loved the game enough and scored runs, he might have the chance to emulate his great hero Vivian Richards and make a hundred hundreds. It became a little bit of a target, it set itself in his mind without him really considering the scale of the achievement should he make it.

Grace was the first batsman to score one hundred centuries in the first-class game. He reached the mark in the season of 1895. It had taken him 1,113 innings and as usual he was so far ahead of everyone else it seemed for a long time as though he might be the only player ever to do it; not Fry, not Ranji, not Trumper or any others of the golden age came near. As the game formalised and the County Championship proliferated and wickets were leavened in favour of the bat, the feat was achieved again in 1913 by Tom Hayward and then again ten years later by Jack Hobbs, who went on to make another 99. Alf Gover's partner in the cricket school Andy Sandham made his in the same year as Wally Hammond. Bradman – who else – got there in the fewest innings, 295. Boycott – who else – became the first man to have made his one hundredth century during a Test match, an Ashes game, what's more, on his home ground at Headingley. Dennis Amiss, who I'd watched resist Michael Holding at The Oval on my first day of Test cricket, made his one hundredth hundred in 1986, and Viv Richards, who had dominated that game and the series and the entire year of 1976, did it in 1988, becoming the first West Indian batsman to hit the mark. It was an English thing, really. Bradman remained the only Australian on the list. There was one Pakistan batsman, Zaheer Abbas, and Glenn Turner of New Zealand. When Graham Gooch joined the list in 1993, he became the nineteenth Englishman on it. What everyone had in common was county cricket. Only in England could you realistically play enough first-class innings to gain the opportunity to score a hundred centuries – either that or you had to be Bradman. But the game was changing. As Graeme Hick and Mark Ramprakash approached the end of their careers, the players good enough to make that many centuries were otherwise engaged. They played international cricket almost full-time. White-ball cricket had grown into the fallow spaces – Sachin Tendulkar, for example, would spend more than a year of his life playing one-day internationals for India. It was clear that if anyone were to follow Gooch on to the list, they would probably be the last to do so.

Yet it remained one of the great Everests of batsman-ship. Leading batsmen passed fifty once every three or four innings, so even the faintest chance to score a century came a quarter of the time, and only Bradman had managed that sort of conversion rate. The average number of innings taken by the men who'd made a hundred hundreds was 801.

Scoring a hundred centuries was a mark of endurance and hunger and desire. It took painstaking dedication, innings after innings, match after match, year after year, through injury and bad form and bad luck and great bowling and poor wickets and bad weather and personal problems and the constant need to keep the demons at bay. That so few people had done it, and that the window to do so was being closed by time and the shifting patterns of the game's structure, made it even rarer and more cherishable. It was a chance to stand alongside Grace and Hobbs and Bradman and Richards and very few others, forever.

On 30 May 1998 at the New Road ground overlooked by Worcester Cathedral and bordered by the Severn, Graeme Hick made his second hundred of Worcestershire's match against Sussex and in doing so became the twenty-fourth man to join the list, and at 32 years and eight days old the second youngest (Hammond had been 14 days younger). It had taken him 574 innings, meaning that only Bradman and Denis Compton had got there more quickly. Four of his centuries had come in Test matches. It's fair to say that of all the players to have made one hundred centuries, Hick was regarded with the most ambivalence. He stood among greats, yet even he was not sure he should be there. The enigma deepened.

2005 had been a bad season for Surrey. They'd been found guilty of ball-tampering and were relegated from division one of the County Championship by a single point. He'd been stand-in captain when it happened, and he felt let down by the behaviour of some of the team. He'd signed up to publish a diary of his season. He thought at the time that it would be a lame, sit-on-the-fence book, but when he started writing he found that a few home truths about some of the players came out. He was angry and upset, so angry and upset that he didn't touch a bat throughout the winter, didn't want to. When the new season came around, Steve Rixon, the coach, had left. Alan Butcher was the new coach and his son Mark was the captain. The first thing Alan Butcher did was sit the squad down and ask if any of them had a problem with his book. He knew that Jimmy Ormond, Mohammad Akram and Ali Brown might. Ormond said that he should have been spoken to personally rather than through the pages of a diary. He knew that he had talked to him, several times during the season, but whatever. It was done. He felt a little better. He began to practise. Butcher left it to him to decide if he wanted to go on the pre-season trip to India. He went, and it began, his great second act.

'I suppose the feeling was that I had created a momentum where things were going my way. A number of things come together, where you've given yourself every chance to be successful. Physically I was in good shape. I knew the grounds well. I had experience. I did my homework on the other players. I felt mentally relaxed. I'd often chat to the umpire at the non-striker's end about football or anything else. I was much better at switching down and switching up. All those things came together. I had a great balance between being really tight and committed to my defensive game, but then when the opportunity arose I attacked with one hundred per cent commitment. As soon as the bowler was off line and length.'

As Ramprakash spoke, it was clear that he'd thought all of this through before, many times. He articulated easily how and why he became the player he became. He had self-knowledge. He spoke quietly but intently. He was obviously used to having people listen to what he had to say. I looked at his hands, which were extraordinary, spade-shaped and heavy, his fingers and the pads of his thumbs thick and muscled from the thousands of hours of gripping and ungripping a bat handle. His eyes remained unreadably dark. He set his watchfulness aside just once when, towards the end of our time, I asked him if he missed batting.

'I do . . . I do . . . big time. The first time we netted here, when we first practised – I was thinking, when is it my turn? The thing about coaching is you give your all to the players. I haven't had that time where I can go over and say, can I have a bat? I'm going to try and make some time. I've got a few oldies games, PCA games. I do still want to play. I still feel I can go out and bat. If I wasn't quite as busy I might well have played for Stanmore. For nostalgia, I've had Gray-Nicolls send me a couple of bats.

'People asked me why I played so long, and I say, well, I enjoyed batting, I enjoyed the challenge. For me to play on till the age of 43, you have to have a love of the game. You can't play that long for money or anything else.' He paused for a moment. 'You know,' he says, 'Alec [Stewart] won't play. He has his reasons. Nasser, Atherton, Thorpe, they don't play. I think it's a great shame . . .'

As the 2006 season was about to start, he made his annual trip down to the Gray-Nicolls factory in Sussex to see John the batmaker and pick out his bats. He pulled one from its wrapper, tapped a couple of balls on it and thought, 'wow, this is going to be good . . .' Handles were his thing. They needed to be perfect, so that he felt his top hand dominated every shot. This one was. When he got hold of it, it felt like an extension of his body, everything was co-ordinated. He could play little push shots that teased the fielder all the way to the boundary, he could hook and pull, he could lash the ball back over the bowler. The weight was right although he never bothered to put it on the scale, didn't need to. It was an amazing piece of wood, it never cracked, barely had a mark on it, it just turned golden brown in the English sun. If Surrey were at home he'd leave it in The Oval dressing-room overnight, but, if they were playing away, he'd take it to the hotel and keep it there, safe beside the bed. It lasted for a season and a half, amazing considering the amount of runs he scored with it, but by the middle of 2007 he noticed that it was starting to wear. They were at the Rose Bowl playing Hampshire and Azhar Mahmood came into the dressing room with this Gray-Nicolls bat, an absolute cracker. 'Where did you get this?' he asked, and Azhar said that Shane Warne had just given it to him. Well, Shane Warne had got the better of him enough times, the least he could do was give him a bloody good bat, so – very unlike him – he marched straight over to their dressing-room and said, 'Shane, mate, I've heard you got some bats . . .' Warne said sure . . . he opened up his locker and let him pick one out, and it was a beauty too.

Through those two seasons he used two bats, two bats for all of those hundreds, all of those runs, two bats for all of his tricks, for everything he'd learned, about batting, about living, about himself. Two bats, and he made them sing.

*

What he did could be expressed numerically. In his time at Surrey, he made 61 centuries in 264 innings – 23.11 per cent of all of his innings were hundreds. From 2002, over nine seasons, he averaged consecutively 56.85, 76.00, 65.16, 74.66, 103.54, 101.30, 61.75, 90.00 and 61.34. In only one of those seasons was his highest score less than 200. On four occasions it was over 250 and on one occasion more than 300. In seven of those seasons he made more centuries than he did fifties: during the years 2007 and 2008 he passed fifty on 21 occasions and turned 16 of them into hundreds. For two entire seasons, in 2006 and 2007, over 49 innings, he was, statistically, due to make more than a hundred runs every time he went to the crease. He was the first man ever to do it, and the first to score 150 or more in an innings in five consecutive matches.

It could be expressed in other ways, too – as the elimination of fallibility; in the beauty of the way he played; for what it meant to him and the people who watched him do it.

'I wasn't thinking about whether it would end or continue,' he said. 'I was living out a process that had evolved over a period of years. If I had got 190 one week, and then I'm playing at Durham, it was all about the next game. I've got to start again. That's why I was consistent. I timed the ball. I didn't really muscle the ball. A lot of my shots I would hit the ball and the fielder would chase it thinking they had a chance but they couldn't quite get there.'

There were so many runs, so many innings, that they had inevitably converged in his mind, coalescing into an impressionistic recall of how it happened, how it felt to bat that way.

'I can remember particular shots if I put my mind to it . . . I remember down at Hampshire, facing Powell, the West Indian, and hooking him . . . At Swansea I got 150, timing the ball well there . . . I can remember bits . . . Lancashire was the last game of 2007 . . . Just the feeling of being pretty relaxed . . .

'It is exciting, because it's great fun. You feel everything is coming really easily. You almost know that the bowler is going to bowl a bad ball, and the fact that you're relaxed means that you play the shots with control. Any quiet periods, you don't fret, you keep it simple. Most innings ebb and flow. I think if I got to thirty it would flash in my mind, there's a hundred here, as long as I didn't go outside of my box, get funky, try and reverse sweep. As long as I contributed, I felt there's a big score here.

'I didn't think about averages. My targets were always quite loose. If I gutsed out 40 or 50 on a difficult wicket, I thought, "yeah, well done", but it also meant that if conditions were in my favour, I was absolutely ruthless. I'd try and get runs in the bank for a rainy day. I got five scores of over 150 in five matches, that was an amazing period. It was almost like I'd created this momentum that would make things go my way. The zone definitely exists. You may only experience it a couple of times in your career. It is a combination of a number of factors which allows you to simply go out and play the game and not think too much about it. All the training you've done puts you in a position where you do the right things. You just watch the ball and react.'

★

After Lord's I went to watch him bat at Wormsley, where he was playing for England Legends against Australian Legends in a T20 game organised by a wine company. He said that he'd been desperate to bat again. The England Legends were fairly recent departees from the pro game: Andrew Strauss, Phil DeFreitas, Matt Maynard, Darren Gough, Phil Tufnell, Devon Malcolm, Andy Caddick, Paul Nixon, Gladstone Small, but the Australians had some of rarer vintage – Jeff Thomson (again), Rodney Hogg and Kim Hughes played alongside Tom Moody, Greg Matthews, Dirk Nannes and Damien Martin. England batted first, and Ramprakash came in at number three. Strauss had opened and he'd already struck a few deferential boundaries from the bowling of Thomson and Hogg, who both shuffled to the crease from a few paces. Ramprakash began scratchily, but by the time he had 14 or 15 runs he was in. He played one extraordinary shot off the back foot, a lofted drive over extra cover with a straight bat that landed just inside the boundary rope, a small miracle of timing and imagination. Like Strauss, he batted respectfully until Australia brought on a young bowler, an 18-year-old kid who was on the field to make up some overs for the old lags. He was a lot quicker than anyone else and in a club game would have had the batsmen jumping around, but for some reason Ramprakash appeared to take exception to his presence. He flipped him to the leg-side boundary two or three times, each one hit harder than the last, and then, as if to fully express his disdain, he dropped to one knee and swept him for four, the sound of the ball cracking from the bat different from everything else hit that day. The shot was utterly dismissive, its message obvious. There was a hint of the Bloodaxe about it. He got to fifty and then, as Strauss had done, contrived to miss a straight one so that someone else could have a go. He walked to the pavilion in that familiar way, slowly pulling off his gloves as he went. Then I saw him standing by the bar, wearing the same expression he adopted at Lord's when people were looking at him, a firm stare directed somewhere in the middle distance.

Early in the 2008 season, he made his ninety-ninth first-class hundred. The next game was at the Rose Bowl, and when he arrived there were about fifteen photographers and a camera crew, but the pitch was a fruity one; he only got twenty or thirty and they all disappeared very quickly once he was out. It was the same at The Oval a few days later, and after another match had gone by, the break for the Twenty20 Cup came along and he had a month without a first-class innings. His next opportunity was at Guildford, on the lovely little out-ground at Woodbridge Road. He got to the game early and was walking out with his pads and gloves for practice when his stomach started hurting. He spent the next hour and half on his hands and knees in the toilet with the worst food poisoning he'd ever had. He had to shout through the door to tell them he couldn't play. He crawled to the physio's room and spent the rest of the day shivering under a blanket. The season went on. It made for great media to question him, just like the England days – was the pressure getting to him? Was he going to crack once again? They made it appear a huge thing. They didn't know the facts – that it had, for example, taken John Edrich 24 innings to go from 99 to one hundred, or that someone else on the list had to wait a year and a half, because hundreds couldn't just be scored to order. His career rate was one every seven innings. This time he went ten. Those ten took three months to happen. Then he went to Headingley, where he had made his first all those years ago, to face Yorkshire. That symmetry once again.

'So I got to 20 and I thought . . . yup.' He smiled at the memory, rubbed those hands together.

'I still had to work very hard for it but I thought I could do it. I felt pretty comfortable, but there was that extra . . . how do you describe it? People would say, are you nervous on 99, but I was excited. You're on the cusp of achieving something wonderful. There was a mix of excitement and perhaps a little bit of extra tension. I remember getting to within one shot of a hundred. It was a left-arm spinner, David Wainwright. He bowled five very good balls, and I'm thinking, "bloody hell . . . give me something".

'I'm trying to be aggressive, but to be fair, he bowled very well. The last ball he put a little bit wider, and I managed to hit the gap. And that was very exciting, a wonderful feeling, having been on this 99 for three months, having had a lot of chat and attention. My mum and dad were there watching.

'I was aware of Graham Gooch, Graeme Hick, Viv Richards [having scored a hundred hundreds]. I actually saw Geoff Boycott hit his four, his on-drive in 1977, I saw that on TV. I have to be honest, to be in that company, of course I'm . . . very, very happy to be on that list. I think it's testament to my dedication and professionalism that I kept myself fit and motivated. But I have to say that all of the other players on that list have achieved great things at international level and I didn't do that. By virtue of the fact that I played through that longevity, I've been lucky. I had to work bloody hard to get up there. I'm level with Viv Richards* – but no way do I compare myself with those players.'

I'd spent a long time wanting to find out what drove him once his international career was over, what made him carry on for all of those quiet afternoons at The Oval, or Guildford, on deserted grounds, in English light, when the world had already made up its mind about him. I'd seen what he had done as something redemptive, but also as something vengeful and angry. It was easy to imagine him as the brooding Heathcliff of the County Championship, an outsider denied his destiny, and perhaps there was an element of all of those things in what happened. But, most of all, it was apparent that great second act of his life was actually inspired by love, the love of what he did and what he had been given.

'It left me with a motivation and a desire to make up for the fact that I hadn't achieved the levels of success that I'd have liked to in international cricket, sure,' he said. 'But why was I doing it? Because it was great fun. I didn't want to be the one back in the dressing-room. That was my fun. If I was not out overnight, I was excited, I couldn't sleep that well. Often I didn't sleep very well because I'd be excited about the opportunity the next day.

*Ramprakash finished his career with 114 first-class hundreds, the same number as Viv Richards. Graeme Hick made 136 – only seven men have scored more, including Geoffrey Boycott, who got 151. Top of the list is Jack Hobbs, with his 199.

'When I got out, I wasn't sated. I would only be disappointed that the enjoyment had ended. That would be my overriding feeling. It's a wonderful time to bat if you get past a hundred. A lot of people get out. I wanted that feeling to continue. By the end, I was happy with my lot. I satisfied a hunger.'

8

Fast Cars Look Fast

Soon after England won the Ashes in 2005, through a combination of strange and fortuitous circumstances, I drove through Snowdonia National Park to a sports centre in the middle of a pretty little Welsh town to bat against Merlyn, the world's greatest bowling machine.

Merlyn was widely thought to have helped England to beat Australia due to its ability to replicate any bowler alive, including England's perpetual nemesis Shane Warne. They'd spent many hours practising against Merlyn being Shane. Merlyn had been built from the parts of an old washing machine by a terrifically entertaining eccentric called Henry Pryor. It was an astonishing achievement. Bowling machines had existed since Nicholas Felix invented the Catapulta, but Merlyn was to cricket what Deep Blue was to chess, a piece of technology that pushed its game beyond the limits of the humans who played. Through the tatty laptop mounted behind its tin body, Merlyn could be programmed to spit a cricket ball at a speed that no man could hit or with spin that no man could impart, with more accuracy than any man had and for longer than any man could do it, just so long as someone remembered to plug it in and drop a cricket ball into the whirring mechanism that rattled within. Henry had to build a special piece of software that made Merlyn randomly bowl some poor deliveries just to ensure that the experience of facing it was relevant.

There was a wonderful Heath Robinson feel to Merlyn. During the Ashes it went from ground to ground in an old horse box, the only mode of transport it would fit in. The part made out of a washing machine was suspended at head height on an iron frame so sturdy it took two men to move it. At the back was a set of steps for the operator to stand on and feed balls into the top of Merlyn's head. It had a kind of traffic light system on the front to indicate when the ball was coming, and a large, blank, unblinking eye in the middle, an eye that stared down the wicket like a dead man's before the ball was fired out from it. On top was a shield that looked like an old car windscreen. Henry called it 'Flintoff's Foil', because he'd bolted it on there to protect the operator from Fred's ferocious straight hitting.

'He really slaughtered it,' Henry deadpanned, '. . . well, when he connected'.

Henry's son Matthew, whose day job was as a journalist on *The Times*, was Merlyn's chief operator, partly because he was fit enough to spend long hours on the step feeding balls in while England players blasted them back towards him, and partly because he and Henry were the only ones who really knew how Merlyn worked.

As soon as I'd seen one or two deliveries I knew that Henry had been touched by a kind of mad genius when he came up with Merlyn. He'd built it in his barn from the washing machine and other bits of old things he had lying around, and yet here was a miracle, every cricketer's dream: a device that could replicate any bowler. It was like something from one of Conan Doyle's short stories.

'In fact,' Henry said quite modestly, 'it can do more than any bowler can. If you wanted to set it up to bowl a ball that turned twenty feet, you could'.

It could also deliver extreme swing at extreme pace – upwards of 100mph. Matthew programmed it, just to show me. The ball came out like a laser, a red blur that screamed into the bottom of the stumps and scattered them yards back into the net. No man could have hit it. We all laughed, because it was the only possible reaction to something like that. Henry had named Merlyn after the Welsh magician of Arthurian legend. It was a fitting tribute. The device was magical, both compelling and terrifying, a 'Jupiter Tonans' to outshine David Harris and everyone since.

I was to face two overs of 'Muralitharan' and then two overs of 'Shane Warne' and then, just to see how Merlyn could swing the ball too, a few deliveries from 'Matthew Hoggard'. I walked to the end of the net. Merlyn's dead eye stared at me. Matthew's head was just about visible behind the Flintoff Foil. Henry sat in a plastic chair beside Merlyn, smiling to himself. Matthew punched the computer pad. The machine began to vibrate deeply, its motors whirring. The traffic light went from red to green. Here came Murali, king of freaky spin . . .

Forget about seeing the ball rotate. You could *hear* it spinning, such was the torque on it. It was whipping around viciously in the air, swirling in a thermal of its own creation.

THE MEANING OF CRICKET

It flew high above the dead eye of Merlyn and high above my eyeline too, as if something underneath was pushing it upwards. It drifted a little in line away from off stump, and then, as it got nearer – and louder – and into its last couple of yards of flight, it dipped, landing a good two feet before it looked like it would. Then it bounced as if it had been thrown into the pitch, leapt upwards again and smacked into my bottom hand before dropping to the floor.

After a few deliveries, it got slightly easier to pick how far it was going to spin (yards) and how high it was going to bounce (higher than you thought possible for an off-spinner to bounce). You could get on the back foot, deep in the crease, and knock it away. You could get right forward and hope it hit bat or pad cleanly. You could, with a horrible fear-sweat creeping down your neck and a feeling that the entire universe was now implacably against you, stay in, on a ball-by-ball basis.

But I was only going to have an experience like this one once, so why do that? Merlyn was programmed to be 'human', after all. And the next delivery looked like a full toss . . . Off I went to meet it. 'Murali' was getting belted . . .

Then it whirred, then it dipped, and then it pitched just in front of me and took off – there's no other description for it – it *took off* from the wicket and launched itself from leg to off, past the bat, past everything, with me stranded halfway down the pitch. There was laughter. There was applause. Matthew shouted one word from the far end. 'Doosra.' Then they started laughing again.

It was absolutely unpickable. It looked like a bad ball till it turned out good. I had faced 'Muralitharan's' doosra, the mystery ball that spun the opposite way to his stock off-break. And just like the great batsmen of the world, I had been done by it. I got then the smallest inkling of what facing the real thing might be like: his crooked run, the little smile, those wide-open eyes . . .

The exact experience of batting against Murali or Warne or any bowler was, of course, only possible in person – the heavy amounts of information that a batsman gains before delivery, key indicators of length, line and pace that come from the run-up and action were denied you. Merlyn had no run-up (although it would have been fantastically cool if he had). Instead there was just the traffic light signal and the dead man's glare.

And yet batting against the machine had its ghostly hints of playing Warne. As Merlyn's washing machine head was brought to the right height for my two overs of 'Shane', I was already facing the mystique that he had created. I wasn't thinking the one simple, pure thought any batsman should think. 'watch the ball.' Rather, what was in my head was something like, 'right, well, the first one will be his stock ball, the huge, drifting leg-break, so don't close yourself off, get your pad out of the way, play it with the bat, don't go hard at it, and whatever else you do, for f**k's sake don't chase it when it turns . . .'

The traffic lights changed. Out sailed the ball in a perfect arc, high and clear. The drift came much later than it looked like it did when I watched Warne bowl on TV, and it was more extreme, too, crossing the width of the stumps from off to leg, burrowing down through the air with late dip. It pitched somewhere around leg and screwed itself into the mat with a pop, spinning back out hard across the stumps, against the direction in which it had come. I'd lunged forward at it, guessing really, and it zipped right past the face of the bat, missing everything. The keeper would have taken it about a stump outside of off, at almost waist height.

This was a different world, with different physics. The thought of an attacking shot was almost laughable. Two overs of it was enough. Two overs of it was exhausting. Facing 'Matthew Hoggard' was a relief.* Driving home, I thought of Kevin Pietersen, who at Lord's on his Test debut in the first match of the 2005 series had launched Warne into the Pavilion benches. The following summer, he would switch-hit Murali for six, and usher in the new age of batting. I understood even more how rare talent was, the distance apart some stood from the rest of us.

Just before I'd left Merlyn to be packed away into his horse box and returned home in triumph to Henry's barn, we'd stood at the end of the net discussing Twenty20 batting. 'What someone needs to do,' I said, thinking of Barry Richards at Fleet, 'is come up with a way of hitting the ball behind the wicketkeeper . . .'

It was a somewhat flippant comment. Twenty20 cricket had only just begun. It was the brainwave of a marketing executive at the ECB called Stuart Robertson, a format that every cricketer had played as a junior but one never considered remotely suitable for the pro game. The first season had come in 2003 and was met with bemusement

---

*By chance, last year I faced the real Matthew Hoggard in the indoor nets at Lord's during a PCA day. He was still rapid and had a horrible, skiddy bouncer that he didn't have to pitch particularly short to make rear up.

by the players, quickly tempered by the delight of appearing in front of the large crowds that arrived almost from day one, drawn by the now obvious pleasure of an entire match contained within a few hours on a summer's evening. By 2005 there had been two international games. In the first New Zealand had worn retro-kit and seventies wigs, and in the second, at Southampton at the start of the English summer, England had thrashed Australia before a packed and raucous crowd, in a game that came to be seen as a harbinger for the Test series. The launch of Lalit Modi's Indian Premier League, with its irresistible synthesis of Bollywood and sport – 'cricketainment,' as Matthew Hayden christened it – was three years away. It would ride the momentum of India's win over Pakistan in the final of the inaugural Twenty20 World Cup seven months beforehand, a victory that did for the shortest format what the 1983 World Cup triumph had done for the one-day game.

It was all still ahead of us in that net in Wales. Twenty20 batting was in its infancy, essentially just a higher-tempo version of the style used in fifty-over cricket. The notion of hitting the ball behind the wicketkeeper came up because it was the only place a batsman could guarantee there would be no fielders. There was no serious thought that it would – or even could – actually be done. Tendulkar was playing a version of Barry Richards' shot to fast, short-pitched bowling, using a horizontal bat to ramp the ball over the slips. A Zimbabwe batsman called Dougie Marillier almost won a one-day international against Australia by moving across his crease to Glenn McGrath and flicking the ball over his shoulder to the fine-leg boundary. But the proof that no shot was beyond the bounds of imagination came in 2009, when the Sri Lankan opener Tillakaratne Dilshan, playing for Delhi Daredevils against Deccan Chargers in the IPL, dropped to one knee while facing the Australian quick bowler Ryan Harris, held the bat out in front of him like a man flipping pancakes and scooped a delivery travelling at 85mph towards his face, dipping his head as he did so to ensure that the ball would make it over his helmet, over the stumps and the wicketkeeper and down to the unprotected boundary.

It was the moment that made clear no part of the ground was safe for the fielding captain.

Between 2005 and 2009, between Merlyn and Dilshan, came the seeds of the greatest technical revolution since Silver Billy Beldham began playing with a vertical bat. This seismic shift was summed up best in four words from modern batting's avatar, India's opener Virender Sehwag. Asked about the approach that had turned him into the fastest scorer in the game, he said simply, 'see ball, hit ball'.

It may have been an off-the-cuff remark, who knows? But it quickly became an irreducibly brilliant philosophy, a credo that Sehwag lived by and that symbolised the times. He was a vision of the future, an outlier. But he became something else, too: mentor, leader, philosopher king. There had always been attacking opening batsmen. Gordon Greenidge, no slouch himself, recalled his partnership with Barry Richards at Hampshire: 'it was not unusual for applause to be ringing round the ground for his fifty while I still had single figures.' Richards once made 325 in a day at Perth against Dennis Lillee among others. Then came Sanath Jayasuriya, Michael Slater, Matthew Hayden, Chris Gayle, Brendon McCullum.

Yet none were Sehwag. Jayasuriya and Hayden had struck Test match triple-centuries. Chris Gayle had made two. But so had Sehwag, and what's more he'd come within seven runs of a third, which would have put him beyond Gayle and Bradman and into history. Hayden and Gayle and Jayasuriya were big men, power players, yet Sehwag's strike rate in Test cricket was 20 runs per hundred balls better than any of them. Sehwag did not have Gayle's shoulders or Jayasuriya's forearms or Hayden's pecs, instead he was an almost implacable little Buddha, soft-edged and pudgy, calmly accepting of the fates whether they swung for him or against. If there was one player he most resembled it was Brian Lara, in that both could hit unstoppably not just for hours but for days. It was they who had built monolithic scores most regularly. Yet Lara didn't open the batting. And he once said that he 'gave the first hour' of his innings to the bowler. Sehwag didn't usually bother giving them the first ball.

His technique was not revolutionary, just thrillingly heightened. What was different was his mind, and the way he saw the game. Where tradition insisted that the new ball and fresh bowlers and aggressive fields were threats to his survival, he saw wide-open spaces and a hard ball that would fly from his bat.

He shared an era with Lara, Tendulkar, Dravid, Ponting and Kallis, yet he was not one of them. As great as they were, they represented the old order, and the way they played was as connected to the past as it was to the future. The game had to move forwards and renew itself. It had to accelerate to match the speed of the culture in which it existed. 'See ball, hit ball' was just the start.

★

Two innings of the same score, 158, became symbolic launch points. The first came from Kevin Pietersen on the final day of the fifth Test of the 2005 Ashes series at The Oval, a fuel-injected, crazily adrenalised counter-attack against the world's best team on a telegenic sun-lit afternoon that transfixed audiences in both countries and beyond. In a thrilling, red-line passage either side of lunch he took on Brett Lee, who was bowling some-where approaching the speed of light, and hooked him repeatedly into the stands, a battle that concluded with Pietersen flat-batting a pull shot almost directly back past the bowler. He would play far more controlled and less chancy innings but that day at The Oval, attitude was all. Over the next five years, England would rise to become the world's number one Test team and win their first ever international competition, the 2010 ICC World Twenty20, with Pietersen's batting – and his lightning rod personality – at the centre of both.

The second was played by Brendon McCullum on 18 April 2008, in the inaugural match of the first Indian Premier League. It was totemic, an innings that made the tournament's failure improbable, if not impossible. His 158 from 73 balls came with 13 sixes and ten fours at a strike rate of 216.43.* Here was batting for the new format and the new century; heightened, spectacular, extreme . . .

---

*Strike rate is calculated as the number of runs a player would theoretically make from 100 deliveries at the rate of scoring they have produced during their innings. Thus someone with a strike rate of 150.00 would be 150 not out after facing 100 deliveries, and so on. As average has less meaning in T20 cricket, strike rate can be used as an alternative measure of the most valuable innings and batsmen.

a nailed-on ratings winner, and a fully realised vision of Sehwag's future. 'See ball, hit ball' had come to represent the acceptance of risk into batting, the willingness to die in order to live.

A decade into franchise cricket, Chris Gayle's employers had included the Barisal Burners, the Matabeleland Tuskers, Sydney Thunder, Royal Challengers Bangalore, West Australia, Kolkata Knight Riders, Jamaica Tallawahs, Somerset and the benighted Stanford Superstars,* and they had value for their coin. If not T20's Bradman, then Gayle had become its WG, its Ranji. In its infant years, he was the conceptual force behind the construction of its batting and its image.

Even to those watching cricket back in the not-so-distant 1990s Gayle would seem like Kubrick's Obelisk, dressed in his space garb, his gold pads and his gridiron helmet, his muscle shirt tight on his giant shoulders, beefed-up bat in his shimmering gloves, a quarter of a billion people watching on TV as his blade scythed at the ball, sending it not just over boundaries, but out of stadiums.

---

*Desperate for an alternative to the IPL, for which it wouldn't release its players who were consequently missing out on a bumper payday, the ECB, led by Giles Clarke, fell for the advances of a Texan 'billionaire' called Allen Stanford. Stanford flew into Lord's by helicopter accompanied by a Perspex box that allegedly contained a million dollars. This was to symbolise the prize for the winners of the Stanford Superstars tournament, a four-team event held in the West Indies, in which the champions would get a million dollars per man. England lost the match, and Stanford turned out to be running a Ponzi scheme that ruined him and his many small investors. He is serving 110 years at a prison in Florida.

One in every nine deliveries that Gayle has faced in T20 cricket has been hit for six. One in *nine*. It feels like a key indicator of how he shaped a format in which no one was at first sure what the prime stats should be. Certainly the side that hits the most sixes usually wins. But even measured in the old-school way, Gayle is getting ahead of the rest by the sort of percentages that Bradman once had. In the history of T20 cricket, Brendon McCullum has made seven centuries, Luke Wright six, David Warner and Michael Klinger five each. No one else, including Pietersen, de Villiers, Kallis, Sehwag and the rest, has made more than three. Chris Gayle has 17, including the format's highest score, 175 not out from 66 deliveries (an innings in which he passed a hundred in 30 balls). In all he has hit 609 sixes – the next best is Kieron Pollard with 388. Even by the blunt tool of batting average, Gayle's mark of 43.90 is way ahead of McCullum at 32, Warner at 33, Raina at 34 and so on.

It would be fascinating to hear him talk about how he does what he does, but he is deliberately enigmatic. His Twitter stream is a flow of emoticons, his Instagram feed a dubious insight into his self-mythologising off-pitch life-style. He rarely gives interviews and, when he does, they tend to yield the wrong kind of headlines. He sees no benefit in demystifying himself, and in truth it is adding to his legend. All we know is what we see from the outside. He is unrecognisable from the beanpole youth who debuted for the West Indies Test team in March 2000, adding pounds of prime beef to his upper body and arms. As he sensed the switch in focus of his life from Test match cricketer to freelance gun for hire, he simplified his method, widening his stance at the crease to provide an immovable base for the carving swings of his bat. But it was not about brute force, at least not always. A closer look at his innings as they evolved showed that he often began more slowly than other players. By the 2012 iteration of the IPL he had the method down. In his 128 not out from 62 deliveries for Royal Challengers against Delhi Daredevils, he didn't score from his first eight deliveries and had ten from his first 17. In his 'berserk' 57 from 31 against Pune, he had four from his first eight deliveries and 17 from his first 16. In his 82 from 59 against Delhi in the match before that, he had two from his first ten and 22 from his first 19; in his 71 from 42 against Kings XI, it was 21 from his first 19; in his 86 from 58 against KKR he had 23 from his first 25. It was a pattern that he began to repeat regularly from then on. Only once he was set would he accelerate, and then with imposing force. Just like Bradman and his rotary method, few copied him. Few had the nerve.

Cricket will reach its agreements with T20, and years from now people will recall its first quaint decade and smile at how old and proper it all looks. A few sages, cryogenically preserved, will be able to say they saw Chris Gayle bat, the new format's Grace, the new format's Bradman. WG would certainly have approved of how little he says, and of how little he runs.

All of the old boundaries, once crossed, seemed to disintegrate, dissolve into the past. Sachin Tendulkar became the first man to score a double-century in a one-day international. Then Virender Sehwag did it. Then Rohit Sharma did it twice. Then Chris Gayle did it during a World Cup.

It meant that Gayle now held a remarkable record, a 3-2-1 that showed mastery of all forms: he'd made a Test match triple-century (two in fact), an ODI double-hundred and a T20 international hundred. Sehwag had almost done it, too: he lacked the T20 international hundred but he had scored a magical and significant one in an IPL semi-final match. Brendon McCullum made the first Test match triple-hundred by a New Zealander. A. B. de Villiers, South Africa's transcendent player and a man as 'variously gifted' as C. B. Fry, batted for ten hours to make 278 against Pakistan in a Test match and scored a 31-ball ODI hundred against West Indies.

What all of this demonstrated was that batting had become not just heightened, but its range had broadened. Its reinvention was a result of physical power and daring and imagination. Kevin Pietersen invented a switch hit, where he turned himself from a right-handed batsman into a left-hander with a standing jump and a flip of his hands. M. S. Dhoni devised a 'helicopter' stroke, a sort of whipped cross-court forehand with a twirled follow-through that sent the ball low and howitzer-like into the stands. Jos Buttler took the Dilscoop and turned it into a new genre of shots that flew the ball not just over the keeper but over the boundary rope, too. Players hit the gym and began filling out their muscle shirts. No one was fat any more, no one wore glasses (except for icy mirror shades). Fielding became some sort of Olympic pursuit, with relay saves, relay catches, bullet throws. In the T20 franchise leagues, the fourth wall between player and broadcaster came down, with batsmen and fielders mic-ed up to offer their own commentary on the game as it was played. In the 2015 Big Bash, Kevin Pietersen was telling TV viewers what shot he was going to hit next ball and then hitting it. Even in club cricket, the biggest change that I have noticed over the time that I've been playing is how hard the ball is now struck.

As an object, the cricket bat changed, too. Not just in the way it was stickered and marketed, but in the way that it looked, the way that it was made and, more significantly, the way that it was thought about. Where it had once been flat and slender and solid, made to last, it became souped up and super-sized, with giant edges and deep bowed blades, drier and lighter and more fragile than ever before.

It was during a drinks break in a game on one of the hottest days of the summer that I picked up Virat Kohli's bat. We were playing at Chalke Valley, a glorious green postage stamp of a ground hidden at the end of a lane by a church near a tiny village in Wiltshire. It was about as far as you can imagine from the fevered bowls of the Wankhede or the Kotla where Kohli scored his runs for India, and the bat had been passed through various, mysterious hands to the player that had it now, the vice-captain of a Mumbai club side called Osian's who were touring England at the same time as the Indian national team.

I played a few air shots with it. What magic did it hold? Had it really been Kohli's? The handle was thick, the blade bone-white. It was a handsome thing, but then so were lots of bats. What set it apart was the contrast between the overall feeling of size and power and the weightlessness of its pick-up. It was almost as if the wood wasn't willow at all, but balsa or some other drier, less dense substance.

★

Chris King trained as a cabinetmaker and antique restorer before spending the next 15 years of his working life as an artist, photographer and university lecturer. He was looking to get back into woodworking when he replied to an opaque advertisement placed by an employment agency for 'a wood craftsman with an interest in sport'. He answered five questions on the phone about cricket ('what's the name of Hampshire's ground? That sort of thing . . .'), then had an interview with the agency and a third interview with Neil Gray and he landed a job that many would covet: as a master batmaker at Gray-Nicolls, the Sussex company that have in the little museum at their factory in Robertsbridge the bats they made for, among many others, W. G. Grace, Barry Richards and Brian Lara. (They also made the noble Scoop with which I scored my first hundred. They can have that one for the museum if they want.)

King had never made a cricket bat, but for a cabinetmaker it is not a complicated object to shape and join. Instead the art of producing a good one is about judgement of the wood and an understanding of its purpose, both physical and psychological. One of the things he realised quite quickly was how misunderstood the product and the process were, not just by fans, but also by ex-players, commentators, journalists, everyone. He'd seen a tweet that I'd sent after picking up Kohli's bat – something about how lightly it must have been pressed to feel the way it felt – and he'd replied saying the way Virat Kohli's bat felt had very little to do with the way that it was pressed, and, what's more, almost everything that people who wrote and talked about 'big bats' and their effect on the modern game was wrong, or at least only half right.

Now we were sitting in the bright showroom at Gray-Nicolls, some new weapons, gleaming and huge, hanging on the walls beside us.

'It's a common misunderstanding that the size of a cricket bat makes a difference,' he said.* 'When we talk about size, we're talking about the physical dimensions of the bat as opposed to the weight or the mass. Because that's where people can get a little bit confused. What we're up against is the belief that a big bat is more powerful than a bat of the same weight that's smaller, which it isn't. That's against the laws of physics.'

For the century or so after Grace and Fry and Ranji led the game into its first golden age, the cricket bat remained essentially unchanged. The shape was simple; a master bat-maker could produce 80 a day. It wasn't until the 1970s that a functional object became something new and desirable, something marketable and memorable. Television played a role. Cricket went through its futuristic shiver with Kerry Packer and bat design got funky. Into the hands of the game's big players came the Gray-Nicolls GN100, aka the Scoop; the Stuart Surridge Jumbo; the Slazenger V12; the Duncan Fearnley Magnum. Dennis Lillee walked to the crease with the aluminium ComBat and got the Laws of the game rewritten.

Cricket bats were transformed into objects of fetish, things to be aspired to, lusted after, cherished. They became associated with particular batsmen and particular

---

*The length and width of bats remains unchanged – the extra size comes in the thickness of the edges and the depth of the bat.

innings. They were part of the iconography of an era. The Scoop and the Jumbo in particular were daring experiments in form, the first bats in history to deviate from the standard design, and the emotional response they produced among their users suggested a psychological element to the relationship between player and bat that had not really been considered before.

But the cricket bat had not yet taken its great leap forwards. Pictures of players from the start of the twenty-first century showed that the object was still traditional, slender-edged and flat-faced. Indeed, the fashion had moved away from hollowed backs and loaded spines to something less outré.

The first intimations of change came in India, where batting was worshipped and many of the most skilled podshavers work with willow shipped from England. Here, at last, the bat began to respond to the psychological urges of the player using it. The blade was given an inward bow; instead of being a flat, sometimes convex surface, it took on a visually pleasing curve. That curve was mirrored on the sides of the bat, where the back edges swooped outwards at the middle. And on bats made for Indian pitches where the ball's bounce was lower, that middle was not really in the middle at all but a few degrees below, giving the impression of deepening power as the player looked down on it.

The extra wood needed to come from somewhere. Older bats like the Jumbo and the Magnum that this new design was starting to dwarf were solid and heavy. The new bats had greater size but their density was different. The moisture content was lower, the pressing less firm, and wood shaved from the shoulders and the first few inches of the blade allowed more for the middle and on the edges. It was an illusion of weight if not size.

To understand the bat, you had to understand the life and death of the wood that it was made from. *Salix alba*, or white willow, is one of almost four hundred species in the *Salix* genus. It is a deciduous tree that likes the damp soils and cold, temperate climate of the northern hemisphere, specifically England, where it can access the volume of water that it needs to feed and grow. Its roots are large and tenacious and take readily. The trunk of *Salix alba* is a complex network of tubes designed to draw moisture upwards to the leaves as efficiently as possible. It is fast-growing and retains large amounts of CO_2, meaning it's often used for biofuel and grown beside motorways to air-scrub pollution. The wood it produces is tough yet pliable, and man has always known it − willow tools have been dated to 8300 BC.

Although other types of the genus, most notably Kashmir willow, have been used to make cricket bats, and other woods with similar density like poplar have been tried, *Salix alba* grown in England provides the wood for every high-grade cricket bat in the world. Its comparative rarity means that the industry, and by extension the sport, is vulnerable to fungi and disease of the kind that caused Dutch elm disease and ash dieback. Some arborealists say that it is only a matter of time before such a plague comes to willow, although no one can say for sure how or when it might happen.

The trees are usually harvested between the ages of 15 and 20 years. The grains that appear on the bat face are the growth rings of the trunk, each one measuring 12 months of outward expansion. The narrower the grain, the less size the tree's circumference has gained in a year, thus bats with a tight grain come from the slowest growing trees. A very dark grain indicates a dry summer – veteran batmakers can still spot a bat that was growing in 1976, the year of that famous and enduring English heat wave.

We walked into the yard to look at some newly felled trees. Up close, the trunks were huge and solid, movable only with heavy machinery. The bark was an inch thick and, when I put my hand on it, damp to the touch. The wood itself was a dark yellow, full of water and sap. It was easy to see why batmakers laughed at some of the more common myths that they heard from their keener customers: that the best willow came from Essex because it's windy out there in the flatlands and wind creates more tension in the wood; or that a rainy year makes more weaknesses in the grain. The trees were thick and heavy and wet; they evolved over thousands of years to thrive in rain and wind and cold.

The trunks were cut into three-sided clefts the rough length of a bat. Still full of moisture, swollen and rough-edged, it took two hands to lift one. They were stacked in high drying sheds, where they began to shrink and whiten as they lost volume and water. When it was finally dried the difference in weight was remarkable. *Salix alba* took on a fibrous, light quality that more dense, slower growing woods could never have.

The judgement of these clefts was the batmaker's primary skill. They lay in their thousands in the drying shed, awaiting a grade that would decide their fate. Gray-Nicolls made 60,000 cricket bats per year. Most of those were shaped in India, where batmakers were more plentiful and demand could be met. The bulk of the clefts would be packed and shipped to the subcontinent. Some came back once they were finished, others journeyed onwards around the world to wherever the game was played. These few English fields and farms supported them all.

'A cleft of willow can vary in weight by a pound or more,' Chris King said. 'Two identical pieces of wood, same grain, cut to the same size, will vary by a pound in an object that weighs four to five pounds. That a big variation in density. And that's not moisture, because they've all been dried to ten or fifteen per cent moisture. It's the density of the fibres in the wood. If people start asking for big bats, you pick the lighter willow. Suddenly the lighter willow is more sought-after, and it's rare. So big, light bats tend to be more expensive because you're making for a select group.'

He pulled a bat from the workshop, a bat that had broken a small piece of his batmaking heart.

'Feel that,' he said.

It felt the same as Kohli's bat – a distinctive, airy lightness. The fine tubes made to suck moisture through the trunk of the willow had less density, giving the wood a quality like balsa, dry and light.

'I found about a hundred clefts [this good] and I used them for the pros,' King said. 'This one . . .' he ran his hand down the bat. 'Almost perfect, isn't it . . .'

The bat went to Gloucestershire's Dan Housego and it lasted 200 runs before a section of the spine split irreparably away. Chris had reattached it with an elastic band, so that I could see the dramatic, sweeping lines that he had shaped.

In my hands was the paradox of the modern weapon: it had become too fit for purpose. The materials and design had been pushed to their limits. Like Formula One cars, they operated at the outer edges of what was possible. Twenty years of growth, the felling, the drying, the shaping, the sanding, the finishing, the eye and the experience and the love, all for 200 runs.

Chris King sighed. 'The average pro bat now lasts between two hundred and one thousand runs. You can get lucky, but that's an average life.'

Every cricket bat is dying, just at different speeds. When the face is pressed, the fibres of the willow are crushed together. About a centimetre of unpressed wood is compacted down to a couple of millimetres to make it hard enough to resist the repeated impact of a fast-moving, hard leather ball. As the bat is used, the fibres that have been pushed together begin to separate in a process called delamination. In the early stage of delamination the bat reaches its peak, when the ball will feel as though it is trampolining from the face.

Sky Sports had asked Chris King to make a series of replica bats for an experiment conducted by Mike Atherton and Andrew Strauss. King made five, each one echoing a different era of cricket from the days of Grace to the present season. Atherton and Strauss discovered that the performance when the ball was struck in the centre of the bat was almost the same in every era. The differences came when the connection was less good, made low down or high up or towards one or other of the edges. While older bats demanded purity, the bats of the twenty-first century were far more forgiving.

In this there was a parallel with golf, where older, bladed clubs required a precise strike while the more modern cavity-backed irons were designed to minimise an amateur's mistakes yet found their way into the professional game. It would be easy to draw a line through the evolution of bats to the increased dominance of the batsmen now laying waste to conventional notions of what batting was. Yet as in golf, once Tiger Woods had begun dismantling the world's best courses by driving the ball more than 300 yards, a new generation of players grew up watching him and began to do the same. Cricket, too, had its outliers: Gayle, Sehwag, McCullum and others. What had changed was intent, the intent to hit the ball harder and further and more often than ever before. Intent fed batsmanship, which fed the change in bats and so on in an endless upward spiral.

The future is not so much in the wood as in the head. The cricket bat has maxed out. It may get a sliver thicker, a hair lighter, but it cannot go much further. Its real developments will come in how it makes its owner feel. Chris King is working on bat designs that appeal to the psyche of the human being looking down on them.

'If I have two bats of the same weight, same grain, that pick up pretty much the same, that sound the same when I knock them up with the mallet, the pro will always choose the one with the bigger edges. Always will. It's psychological.'

King had designed a bat called the Nemesis, which looked like a sleek and futuristic version of the Jumbo, with a shape like a car spoiler low on its spine, and the Omega, a bat with soft curves and ellipses like the lines of muscle, a bat made to lift the spirits and the ego of the player holding it.

He wanted to incorporate that psychology into his future engineering, too. 'I thought, "right I'm going to make something that looks like it's going to put the ball over the boundary, that looks like it'll destroy the bowler". To make something that looks aggressive.

'In the end,' he said, 'fast cars look fast, don't they . . .'

9

Time Slows the Rapid Eye

Tony Shillinglaw was 15 years old when everything changed. It was 1954, and he'd just been selected to open the batting for North of England Schoolboys in a match against the South. He was a natural player, a street cricketer when such a thing still existed in England, but the coaches got hold of him and said that they didn't like his stance or the way that he held his bat with a closed face, and that he'd have to listen to them if he wanted to get anywhere in the game.

It would be 45 years before he changed back again. During that time he did get somewhere. He dismissed John Edrich and Ken Barrington in a Gillette Cup tie in 1964, playing for Cheshire against Surrey, and at Birkenhead Park CC he became a club legend. Yet after just an hour or so in his company, his eyes blazing like a prophet's, it was obvious that he felt his chance in cricket had been wasted. It had just taken him the best part of five decades to work out why.

We were at the indoor school in the back of the pavilion at Birkenhead's pretty parkland ground. Outside it was one of those warm, grey summer Sundays when the clouds feel low enough to touch. There was a wedding party in the main hall, the lads in their sharp shirts and box-fresh trainers, the girls with glowing spray tans and vertiginous heels. Tony Shillinglaw had marched past them with barely a glance. In his hand was a blue plastic cricket bat and a bucket with balls of various shapes and sizes: a golf ball, hard, rubber bouncy balls, plastic cricket balls and so on. He opened up the indoor nets, turned on the lights, pulled a tennis ball from the bucket and began striking it, with one continuous flowing movement of his arms and feet, up against the breezeblock wall of the school.

He was a small man but lithe, and he moved with the ease and economy of the natural athlete. It was hard to believe, watching him, that he was 78 years old. As he batted, he talked unceasingly about what he was doing and why he was doing it. His voice was punctuated by the rhythmic clump of the tennis ball on the wall bouncing around the nearly empty hall.

He stopped quite suddenly, picked up a set of yellow plastic stumps and invited us to bowl at him using the variety of balls in the bucket. He cut and pulled and drove at all of them, the tiny rubber balls flying away, the golf ball skittering across the hard floor. The blue plastic bat made an empty thud every time he connected.

'Your bat speed is fast . . .' I said

'Ah!' he said, his eyes alive once more, 'that's because of the continuous movement, you see! Don't hit at the ball, hit *through* it! The ball itself tells you where to hit it! All you must do is control it! Continuous movement, you see!'

Continuous movement, or, as Shillinglaw had christened it, 'the Rotary Method', had been employed in cricket before, most notably and deliberately by Don Bradman. Tony Shillinglaw's question for the rest of the game was why no one else had ever used it or taught it or even really thought about analysing it. It was a question that had taken him 20 years of research even to begin to answer.

He saw Bradman as the sport's great lost opportunity, a fork in the road not taken. The thought had obsessed him. He wrote a book, 2003's *Bradman Revisited*, and a follow-up paper. He went to Bowral and lectured at the Bradman Museum. He held in his own hands the bat with which Bradman scored 100 runs in three eight-ball overs at Blackheath in New South Wales.

He had an analogy from another sport that began to explain his mission.

'At the 1968 Olympics, Dick Fosbury used the Fosbury Flop to win the Gold medal and from then on, anyone that wanted to win at high jump had to use his method. And Fosbury himself said, "My mind wanted me to get over the bar, and intuitively figured out the most efficient way". Bradman solved the problem of controlling a bouncing ball in his childhood completely intuitively. He developed a different style of batting which took it to unprecedented heights. The difference between him and Fosbury is that nobody copied Bradman.'

★

He held out the blue plastic bat and showed me how to hold it using Bradman's grip. For someone who had always played in an orthodox fashion it was deeply uncomfortable, the thumb of the bottom hand turned right over until it pressed hard against the front of the handle, the left wrist twisted fully around and shutting down the bat face so that, in a normal stance, the leading edge was facing the bowler. Picking the bat up from that position automatically moved it out towards gully, from where Bradman's bat began its looping downward journey.

The style has its root in that childhood game played at Bradman's home in Bowral where, for countless hours, he struck a golf ball with a cricket stump as it rebounded from the family water tank. 'Looking back,' Bradman wrote many years later, 'I can understand how it must have developed the co-ordination of eye, brain and muscle that served me so well.'

'What he means when he says muscle,' Shillinglaw said in his animated way, 'is not just hands and feet but his whole body. From the minute he picks up his bat, which rotates his shoulders, it begins a chain reaction of a synchronised response to the sight of the ball. A man in the *Sydney Morning Herald* once wrote that it wasn't as if Bradman was better than other people at doing the same thing . . . What Bradman was doing is different . . .'

These movements were the crux of Tony Shillinglaw's obsession. Unravelling them had taken him more than 20 years. It began when he went into the garage of his bungalow a mile or so from the cricket ground, cleared some space and replicated as closely as he could the conditions under which Bradman played his childhood game. He had the advantage of his own natural grip and stance but it was a battle, a war even, between his intellectual conviction that the method could be reproduced and his physical limitations. When Dick Fosbury had flopped backwards over the high-jump bar the difference in what he had done was obvious, even to people who'd never been anywhere near a high-jump pit. Bradman's difference emerged over the years in which he dominated batting, and it was an era without deep technical analysis or biomechanics. All that still existed of Bradman's technique was the newsreel, an instructional video and his written and spoken words. It needed to be unpicked painstakingly. After a while Shillinglaw could replicate Bradman's game using the plastic bat and a tennis ball but it took supreme concentration to do so for very long. The effort required to get the bat back into position quickly enough to hit a ball rebounding from 8ft away was draining. The breakthrough came when he remembered Bradman's words on the importance of a full follow-through on every shot. Suddenly, instead of stabbing at the ball and hurriedly withdrawing the bat for the next shot, he flowed right through, the action widening his shoulders and, as he wrote in *Bradman Revisited*, 'setting mind and body free to respond to the sight of the ball'.

At the age of 60 he took the Rotary Method into club cricket and began to bat with it. 'Too little and too late for my career, but not too late to realise that all those years ago I made a great mistake in changing my early successful schoolboy style. Unfortunately for me I didn't have the Don's resolution but at least I know now how he did it and, given the right dedication, that it can be successfully copied.'

There is a theory that the Rotary Method actually reduced Bradman's need to concentrate. Because his technique was fluid and less demanding on the body than more artificial 'straight bat' movements, he tired less easily. And because he had trained himself to react instinctively to the ball, his need for 'conscious' concentration may have been less.

'When you transfer the Rotary Method from a space of about eight feet to the twenty-two yards of a cricket pitch, the action is less frenetic,' says Shillinglaw. 'And Bradman didn't used to move at all until the ball was delivered. No trigger movements or anything like that. He turned batting into a subconscious act.'

By now we had decamped to the Shillinglaw living room for tea and cakes. Brian Hale, Shillinglaw's co-author and co-traveller on this two-decade odyssey to understand Bradman, sat quietly while Shillinglaw talked on, a position he seemed quite used to. Since Tony Shillinglaw's wife Eve passed away in 2014, the quest to evangelise the Rotary Method had filled even more of his time. It energised him in a way that few things energise few people. Brian Hale smiled gently as he listened to his friend telling stories he has heard hundreds of times before. We talked about other people who have studied Bradman: Tim Noakes, the South African researcher who worked closely with Bob Woolmer on the theories behind how cricketers saw the ball, used Tony's research in *Bradman Revisited* to write a section on Bradman in *Bob Woolmer's Art and Science of Cricket*.

The book was almost finished as Woolmer prepared to take the Pakistan national team that he was coaching to the World Cup in the West Indies. At their last meeting before he left, Tim Noakes showed Woolmer a collection of pictures he'd assembled which demonstrated that some of the game's greatest players had naturally incorporated part of the Rotary Method into their techniques.

'Well, Tim,' Woolmer had said, 'we need to look at this as soon as I return from the World Cup.'

Bob Woolmer never did. He died suddenly at his hotel in Jamaica soon after Pakistan had been eliminated from the tournament. Police opened a murder investigation and then declared that he had died from natural causes. The coroner recorded an open verdict.

Brian Hale also recalled seeing Bradman in the flesh in 1948; uppermost in his memory is the way the crowd roared in a way he'd never heard before as Bradman walked to and from the wicket. 'There was the feeling that we were watching a one-off genius.'

Were they? Bradman passed through cricket like a comet across the heavens, rare and distant. Was his real message lost somewhere in the miles that separated him and everyone else? In the report that Shillinglaw and Hale published as a follow-up to *Bradman Revisited*, they listed some of Bradman's own views on helping batsmen.

'Coaching should deal with what to do with the ball, not so much how to do it', runs one.

And 'Better to hit the ball with an apparently unorthodox style than miss it with a correct one.'

And 'Watch others, note their methods and learn by observation and example.'

His few terse sentences of advice contained something with which Tony Shillinglaw had connected on a deep level. Tony Shillinglaw knew that his work was not done. At the indoor school he coached young players, who could watch the man who bats like Bradman hit ball after ball against the wall with his blue plastic bat. In South Africa, Tim Noakes continued to research Bradman, too. One of his PhD students is attempting to demonstrate that Shillinglaw's theory of the Rotary Method is correct, and they are becoming convinced that it is. Noakes' work with groups of young cricketers in Cape Town has confirmed that those who are uncoached tend towards Bradman's technique naturally. It is only when conventional coaching takes over that their methods become altered. More definitively, they are testing the theory that while a conventional technique will produce a good batting average up to and including first-class level, in international cricket and particularly in white-ball cricket, the closer a technique matches Bradman's the higher the average that will result.

Perhaps one day a new Don will walk through the door at Birkenhead Park CC or Cape Town University and cricket will be reconnected with the big-time game-play of its greatest star. Or maybe the Rotary Method will reappear in someone who can advance the form, make it new for batting's new age and steer the game back down its path not taken. But the real lesson that Tony Shillinglaw was teaching seemed to be to his 15-year-old self, who lost his way before he'd really begun.

★

Cricket seemed inexhaustibly varied, but then once so had chess. Then came machines that could defeat grand masters. Computing grunt gave weight to the notion that chess could not only be calculated to positions beyond those that the human brain could hold, but perhaps to the end of the game itself. It may take quantum computing power to do it, but theoretically it was a finite thing. It was solvable.

When Andy Flower became England coach, he read a book given to him by the man he'd taken over from, Peter Moores. It was called *Moneyball*, and it was about a bunch of baseball card geeks who'd discovered that lots of the statistics, or metrics, that the sport used to evaluate players were the wrong ones and for a while the Oakland As, an unfashionable franchise, put together a winning team on the back of this competitive advantage. Now every sport was searching for its Moneyball moment and at their base at Loughborough University the ECB performance programme were crunching stats like never before. Every available match in every format was analysed and broken down and truths began to emerge. Flower, bright and taciturn, gave little of it away but one of his favourites of the early revelations was that the team that scored most singles in an ODI usually won, while the team that scored most singles in a T20 match usually lost. What it meant was that England could begin to set their infields closer and try and shut down easy singles in ODIs, especially once they had analysed where most of the singles were scored from each of their bowlers. In that way cricket became more formulaic, or at least more prescribed (by the time of the disastrous Ashes tour of 2013–14, on which England had taken a 19-page diet sheet, Gideon Haigh wrote of them: 'they are a team that controls the controllables, achieves the achievables and eats the edibles').

Everyone else did it, too, and soon professionals were living even more examined lives. Every moment they spent on the field and their performances during training were logged and analysed and fed back to them via video and analytical computer programmes like Hawk-Eye. Some liked it and some didn't – that was pretty much dependent on their personality type (which was also tested and fed back to them). Flower led England through their most successful period of recent times, and yet the game, by the end, moved ahead of him in a way that no numbers could have predicted. He left at the end of that Ashes tour, which was lost 5-0 and cost England the services of Graeme Swann, who retired, and Kevin Pietersen, who was sacked and then, in scenes probably last seen in the days of Trueman and Boycott, was re-sacked again a few months later on the day that he scored a triple-hundred for Surrey. The following winter came a 50-over World Cup won by Australia but lit up by Brendon McCullum's New Zealand: his attacking zeal as batsman and captain finally transporting everything learned about T20 cricket to a longer format. England were not just eliminated, they were humiliated: they were like the Monty Python character who tried to win a gunfight with a banana. After the catastrophic loss to Bangladesh that sent them home, Peter Moores, who had returned as coach in place of Flower, said England would have to 'look at the data' to see what had happened in the game,* a remark that was widely lampooned and that symbolically marked the end of the sport's first phase of statistical analysis. Cricket seemed somehow resistant to predictability, even under some serious number-crunching power and a large investment of time and resources. Somewhere within it was human mystery. England's lead statistician Nathan Leamon became fascinated with one of the game's most fundamental questions: was winning the toss an advantage? His results were ambiguous: sometimes it was obviously, but often it wasn't, and what actually happened bore little result to what cricketers thought had happened. He spent some time trying to answer another question: whether it was possible to predict when a player was in terminal decline, whether a downward spiral of results was apparent.

It wasn't.

Everything did finish, though. Everything ended and Kevin Pietersen's dismissal felt to me like one of the saddest endings. I'd become invested in his batting; he was on the list with Barry Richards, Geoffrey Boycott, Mike Atherton, Mark Ramprakash . . . He'd brought me back to the game after a brief interregnum when it faded a little. That was in 2004, when he first got into the England one-day side and hit three centuries against South Africa in South Africa while the entire crowd seemed to be against him. He was

---

*Moores was probably slightly misquoted, and was said to have received an apology from the BBC over its reporting of his comments. He said that England had relied so little on 'data' at the World Cup that their lead statistician Nathan Leamon was on the verge of leaving the tour. Leamon has one of the better nicknames on the circuit – the players call him 'Numbers'.

a classic exile, desperate to fit in but determined to stand out. His batting was unorthodox and thrilling. As his days with England careened along, all absurd highs and crashing lows, he became part of the reason that I started a blog. I had a career – of sorts – as a writer, in as far as I had somehow been able to scrape a living at it, but I'd never written about cricket. It seemed like a busman's holiday. Then I decided to do it anonymously – not because I was under any illusions of fame or renown (I didn't have any) but because then it could be something that was purely about fun, written only when I wanted to write, with only what I wanted to write about. I looked online to see what was out there and was met immediately with a vast clamour of voices, funny, wise, mad, urgent, laconic, obsessive, combative, all of them entirely unconcerned with what anyone thought of them as writers but instead driven to say what they had to say about the game.* It seemed democratic and unmediated, a place free of the conventional wisdom of conventional voices. The blog reconnected me to cricket and as I wrote I started to articulate what it had meant to me. Pietersen became one of its recurring subjects. He was as quirky as the game itself, his fortunes capricious, his greatest innings played at an emotional pitch that he could reach only rarely. The world saw him as an egotist but he wasn't, at least not in the way they thought. Norman Mailer had nailed what ego in sportsmen really was back

---

*This was in 2008, in the glory days of blogging, i.e. pre-Twitter. The best, and for me most influential, of all of them was Jarrod Kimber's Cricket With Balls, which approached writing about the game in an entirely new way, with a mad energy that seemed lacking in almost every weary piece of newspaper reporting or commentary box cliché.

in 1970 when he was writing about Muhammad Ali: 'to declare that we are sure of ourselves when we are not.' That was perfect, and perfect for Pietersen. He was introverted and insecure, desperate for approval rather than attention.*
What he could offer in return was this extraordinary talent that itself seemed fragile and enigmatic but that could help him to win cricket matches in a way that few people could. At the root of his insecurity, I thought, was something that made Pietersen unique among the world's top batsmen. When he'd come to England at 22 years old to play club cricket for Cannock, he was an off-spin bowler who batted a little. Five years later he was playing Test cricket in England's top order. Unlike the other big-name batters of the era, the discipline was not rooted in his childhood; he had not come up through the system as a nascent superstar.

I suppose I related to that. In one way pro batting was a bit like pro writing: there were no guarantees, and it could finish at any time. A bad trot could mean the end. Pietersen made me wonder why insecure people were attracted to things that offered no security. On the night that he was sacked by England, 5 February 2014, without even thinking about why or what I was going to write, I sat down and blogged:

Last year a writer I liked very much died. Jonathan Rendall published three books, one of which,

*The captain Pietersen most enjoyed playing under was Michael Vaughan, who said of him: 'KP is not a confident person. He obviously has great belief in his ability but that's not quite the same thing . . . And I know KP wants to be loved. I try to text him and talk to him as often as I can because I know he is insecure.'

Twelve Grand, is among my favourites by any author. He was a boozy, melancholic soul with a low-lit style and his obituaries didn't hold back on his dissolute, sometimes chaotic life. His writing was admired by Tom Stoppard and he won a Somerset Maugham prize but almost every piece on him noted his 'wasted talent', partly because he had died so painfully young. Well he didn't seem to have wasted it to me.

It's the nature of talent, when it manifests itself as apparently effortless brilliance, for it to appear both ephemeral and carelessly used by the characters who possess it. Yet the life is inseparable from the art, indeed the art is art because it is informed by the life. Jonathan Rendall couldn't have written the way he did without being the person that he was, and it's analogous that Kevin Pietersen could not bat in the way that he does without being the man that he is. The talent might appear different because those of us with lesser ability imagine ourselves guarding it jealously, rationing it out, tending it like a secret garden.

In 2004 I had become distant from the game. I'd lived in Australia for a while, hadn't played much, just about kept up with it in the papers. It had receded in my interior life. I was in my lounge one morning, the sun was out, I was struggling to write something or other and I realised that England were about to play South Africa. The area had cable and I had a bit of money, and before I really thought about it, I was on the phone getting

Sky Sports turned on. In the couple of hours that it took, I realised that I felt more excited and happy than for a while. The game was back. I didn't know why, but I could feel it.

That was the series when Pietersen played his three extraordinary one-day innings, centuries struck at an emotional pitch as true as a tuning fork. At the time, and right through until the following summer, he was talked about as a one-day player with a technique too iconoclastic for Tests but I knew with a rare certainty that it wasn't true. He hit 92 in a game at Bristol and the wave he was making became irresistible. The story was that he was picked [in the Test team] over Graham Thorpe, but really the choice was between Thorpe and Ian Bell. After Bristol, Pietersen was playing either way.

Lord's was extraordinary. England were hammered but on the first morning the bowlers roughed Australia up and each time Pietersen batted he murdered Shane Warne. It was obvious from the way he walked out how much he wanted it.

From that game on, I was more invested in his batting than in anyone else's. Something was happening, not just to England, but to the way the game was played. There were some batsmen more skilled and better than Pietersen in that phase, but he had this innate imagination and feel. His game was an act of creativity and it's no exaggeration to say that he broadened the horizons of batsmanship.

He wasn't playing in isolation of course. The game was changing – he arrived, essentially, at the same time as T20 – and Virender Sehwag was pushing at the limits too, along with Chris Gayle and Adam Gilchrist and then lots of others. There was a kind of kinship between them. They were not formal heroes like Tendulkar or Dravid or Ponting, and their effect on the future would be different.

But KP was English, or at least he was playing for England, and the English psyche, deeply conservative, deeply repressed, is a challenging place for the non-conformist. It was doomed from the start and I knew it. In a way, it's amazing that he lasted as long as he did.

It's fair to say he was part of the reason for starting this blog. Once he had commanded the imagination, it was hard to resist writing about him, because in working out what he was doing, I was often working out what I felt I knew about cricket, or what it meant to me.

When a player like Pietersen or a writer like Jonathan Rendall comes along, it's easy to develop a relationship with their work that leads you to think that you know more about them than you do. All you really know is that their talent speaks to you in some way.

Twelve Grand seems like an effortless book, and yet Rendall worked so hard on it he was briefly hospitalised. As Kevin Mitchell wrote of him, his love affair with writing 'ebbed away' after that. Pietersen trained and practised harder than anyone: the imagination demanded it. Nothing good can be effortless at that level.

I've found it quite hard to care about the arguments over who's done what and what went wrong that have raged today. Four men sat in a room and brought things to an end, and I think in years to come it will be a burden on them, maybe not publicly but when they have to be alone and remember it. If Pietersen hadn't been reintegrated, then we would not have had Mumbai, perhaps his greatest innings and one of the best of the modern era. So what will we not have now?

Overwhelming talent wants us to think it's wasted because, along with being apparently effortless, it seems somehow endless, inexhaustible. It works on the imagination. Pietersen's career will never be seen as complete, and he will have to live with hearing about it. His talent has not been wasted though. It's better to write three good books and leave 'em wanting more. Pietersen's legacy is not one of numbers, but what his batting has meant to those who have watched it.

For a while now I've wondered if he'll be remembered as a great player or a player of great innings. It doesn't matter. He will be remembered. He will live.

Barry Richards got the same thing about 'wasted' talent. I didn't know it at the time, but that day at Fleet CC would be among his last on a cricket field for Hampshire, or for anyone. He played six games the following season and although he eked out a couple more years in South Africa in the Currie Cup, he was gone almost from that moment. For Christmas in 1978 I got his autobiography, *The Barry Richards Story*, and began to understand how he could write a sentence like: 'When I walk off a county ground for the last time . . . it will be with an enormous sense of relief.' He had played four Test matches before South Africa's exclusion began, all against Australia. In seven innings, he made two centuries, two fifties and averaged more than 70. He was 24 then, and impossibly good, and he was probably only genuinely challenged once more in his career, when he was in his thirties and 'on the decline' – his words – and went to play in Kerry Packer's World Series Cricket. He made more than five hundred runs in five games for the World XI. Against Australia in the second 'Supertest' of 1978 he got 207, and for 90 minutes of that innings he batted with Viv Richards, then nearing his peak. Barry made 93 to Viv's 41.*

I never saw him bat again and there is very little footage available of him playing, even now. And yet for me and for so many others who were there on the boundaries of cricket grounds while he did, however fleetingly, he lives indelibly in the mind's eye: a legend, a wizard, a true star. Tales of his talent are legion. He once imagined the ground as a clock face and hit each ball of the over for four to a different point, in clockwise order. He played out an over in a club match in Durban using the edge of his bat (and that was when edges were as slender as an After Eight mint). Nine of his 80 first-class hundreds were scored before lunch. *Nine.* Don Bradman said Richards

*There have been several attempts to have the statistics from World Series Cricket added to the records of those who played – the cricket was certainly of Test standard – but they remain unofficial.

was as good as Jack Hobbs. John Arlott wrote of him as 'a batsman of staggering talent'. His reputation became such that stories of him getting fed up and giving his wicket away, or, as his enduring on-field opponent and good friend Robin Jackman once observed, acquiring 'a convenient groin strain' in the last week of June so that he could watch Wimbledon on TV, added to the idea that what was left of the game could not tax him, and even bored him. That is what was lost to Test match cricket. 'It really hurts him,' Jackman said. 'When you're that talented you want the world to see it, not a few guys watching at Southampton.'

A fluke of birth gave Richards his ability, and another ensured that he was born out of time. We can never know what would have happened had he played more Tests. We will never know how many people of similar potential were born in townships and never had the chance to lift a bat. There is simply no equivalency to any of it. Barry Richards missed out on some games of cricket in a struggle that was infinitely wider and more significant than any one person, or any sport. He had no choice in his sacrifice, either. Had he made it himself, it might have felt easier for him.

He has been called 'the world's most romanticised cricketer' and it's true. Into the space where his Test career might have been has gone myth and imagination. In a fashion, this has conferred the greatness that might have arrived another way. He is entwined with South Africa's past, and they cannot be unwound. His is one story of very many. It feels okay to acknowledge the joy and sadness his batting brought, and that will always arouse difficult and very human emotions. I've often thought that if I could see one day's cricket again, it wouldn't be any of the Test matches or one-day games, or even the two World Cup finals that I watched at Lord's. It would be that innings at Fleet, an innings that Barry Richards no doubt forgot as soon as he was in his car, but which for me began it all and that I return to again and again.

Richards is 70 now, which somehow seems impossible. Time does that, comes along and fucks you up while you're not looking. Alf Gover retired in 1989 and the school was knocked down soon afterwards. He carried on living in the house next door, and before his death at 93 in 2001 he assumed the title of the world's oldest surviving Test cricketer. On the site of the school is some upmarket housing, but I still half expect to see it there every time I drive past, and I wish that I could. It seems odd that it exists now only in the mind, but still feels so tangible and real.

The past only ever got bigger, and the bigger it got the more I understood the process, this ongoing reckoning. Through my blog I met and joined a team of writers, who are just the same as almost every team I've played in – ardent, deluded, funny, unreliably skilled – but they are something else, too: they're old. Or at least, they're older. We have fielded at least one eleven with every player over the age of 40. We're most likely older than every team we play. I see the same look on the faces of the kids in the opposition that I used to have myself: it says 'why are you still doing this?' Last year we went on tour to Italy. We played a team from the Rome league (and faced 'the fastest bowler in Rome' – what a marvellous title to have) and then a Vatican XI (which consisted of seminarians from Sri Lanka and Pakistan, all of them young and rapid and probably faster than Rome's fastest bowler)* in Twenty20 matches on consecutive days. There's no hiding place in T20 cricket. The first game was competitive. The second was a massacre. It took me two weeks to recover. We played a two-day game against an Indian touring team (where I'd held Virat Kohli's bat) on the hottest days of the summer, and survived the second by hosting a two-and-a-half-hour lunch interval at the local pub. But what we have alongside the twanged calves, the thrown-out shoulders, the dodgy eyes and the screaming hamstrings, the miracle cures, the chiropractors and the endless packets of ibuprofen, is camaraderie and friendship, humour and genuine pleasure in one another's occasional successes. Along, of course, with the usual feuds, fallouts, in jokes and misplaced banter . . . With it have come many hours of fiercely contested, inconsequential cricket on some of the loveliest grounds in England. We have played at Wormsley, on Getty's Chilterns estate, where red kites circle above the wooded hills; at Sheffield Park, where a tree once struck by a mighty WG six still stands beyond the boundary; at the Valley of the Rocks and Chalke Valley; Ascott House and Pylewell Park; at Avebury, just beyond the stone circle, and Frogmore, under

*Seminarians go to Rome from countries that lack the funds to train their priests at home. A lot of young men arrive knowing no one, and so they play lots of sport, primarily cricket and football, because it has no language barrier. Our match was a return fixture: the current score is God 2, Authors 0.

Windsor Castle; at Barkby, with its seven trees inside the boundary lines and at Kirkby Portland, where Harold Larwood learned to bowl. We've played three times at Hambledon, and had lunch at the Bat and Ball, from where Richard Nyren dispensed his own gut-busting fayre. And in what is probably the greatest day I have had on a cricket field, we played in the ancient and revived Authors versus Actors fixture on the Nursery Ground at Lord's.*

It was a glorious afternoon. The wicket was hard and true, the boundaries were small and the ball ran over the outfield like a marble on glass. There was a moment in the field when I looked through the gap in the stands beneath the media centre out at the main ground, the light falling down in sheets onto the outfield and the old Pavilion beyond, and I thought 'remember this. . . .'. Remember this because very few people on earth will ever get the chance to do it.

As I got older I understood that the game turned its face towards me all the while. There was an invisible boundary that you crossed when you passed the age at which professional cricketers retired, when things seemed different. All pretence had gone. I may have once been able to imagine a ten-year-old opening for England, but a 45-year-old? Yet this was part of cricket's genius: it had

---

*The Authors had last played the Actors at Lord's in 1912. Conan Doyle and Wodehouse turned out for the Authors, and C. Aubrey Smith, who played one Test for England, for the Actors. Our crews were far more motley, although it's obvious why the fixture was played so often and survived so long: it's hard to think of two 'professions' in which the participants have so much time on their hands.

something for everyone. I still wanted to do well, but I no longer had that sharp and hungry look that I saw in the eyes of good young players, their certainty of movement and absolute commitment. The ball was still hard, the bowling still tough, but the game was more gentle. Where I'd once loathed fielding, now those hours in the sun on perfect grounds passed happily and in the company of friends. And the other year I faced a probing opening spell of 12 overs from a 62-year-old seam bowler who still glared ferociously at me when I played and missed.

There is always hope.

On an April morning four years ago, I'm not really sure why, other than it was the start of the season and his name had come into my head, I Googled Simon Massey. I knew he'd be playing somewhere, because he always was. The first result was a notice of his death at 50 years old, just a few months before. I don't suppose I had seen Simon for ten years and it had been many more since we'd played together, but the time didn't feel like distance. Sitting in front of that screen with its unwanted message, the memories became almost overwhelming. Bloody sad, too.

His early hero was Tony Greig. A while back I'd been through some old boxes in the loft and I found a cricket magazine that he'd made for a school project and photocopied so that he could sell down at the club. It had a pencil drawing he'd done of Greigy on the cover, playing a drive in those SP mitten gloves he used to wear and that I'd coveted until I got a pair.

He'd stayed at Hampshire for two or three years and after the Day of the Pig life slowly took us in different directions, but I always felt like I would run into him again. The few times I did, we picked up exactly where we left off. He didn't make it as a first-team pro, although he'd also played briefly for Northants and then Berkshire in the Minor Counties Championship. I always thought he was unlucky. His off-spin, which I faced a lot, wasn't even the best part of his game to me. He was a tremendously powerful batsman before that kind of hitting was really in vogue, and he could bowl all kinds of seam and swing, and field brilliantly, too. Most of all, though, he was wrapped up in it. I don't know how he felt when he finally had to let it go, but I can imagine, and I know he gave it everything while he could.

I looked at some of the online messages left by the teams he played for. It was obvious that no one could have loved the game more. He made an impression everywhere he went, for his fearless cricket and off-field jokes.

I found a story on the Cricinfo website from 2006 about Henry Allingham, who was 109 years old and the last man alive to have seen Grace play. He'd returned to The Oval for the first time in 103 years to mark the occasion. In the picture, there were a couple of guys holding on to Henry's arm, and one of them was Simon. I don't know how he came to be there, but he deserved that, being one degree of separation from the great Doctor. They were both cricket men.

I wrote a blog about him that his mum and dad saw, and I spent an afternoon with them at their house, surrounded by scrapbooks and cricket magazines. We looked at pictures and reminisced: those mad drives home from Alf's, the strange little orange-flavoured cakes we used to make in his mum's kitchen to take down to the net at Fleet with us, the time he had an ill-conceived perm (he looked like a glory-era Kevin Keegan, just a decade too late), the notices he put up around town for the summer coaching courses he ran, with 'ex Hampshire player' on them and a picture of him – that was typical of Simon, too. His mum told the story of his trip to see the live show of the *Little Britain* TV comedy: he went dressed as one of the female characters 'because everyone would be doing it' and got to the Hammersmith Odeon to find he was the only one that had. He stayed anyway. He'd become a playing member of MCC and had started coaching at The Oval when he was diagnosed with a brain tumour. He knew that he was going to die and he accepted it. For his funeral he recorded a message played to the congregation. He said he'd enjoyed his life, and was happy with everything he'd done. I thought that was one of the bravest things I'd heard of.

A few months later, Darren Gough brought his charity team down to Fleet for a match in memory of Simon and Alex Bolt, another young man who'd died from brain cancer. Facing Gough's XI was a side made up of players from many of the teams that Simon had represented. It was a blue planet afternoon, just as it had been when he'd played there against Barry Richards all those years ago. I went and stood in the same spot that I'd stood in then, over by the practice net, under the trees that Richards had cleared when he hit one onto the pitch and putt course. The boundaries were once again ringed with people. Goughy bowled fast and hit the ball a long way. You could tell he still loved the game, still loved to play. It was a sad, sweet day that finished too soon, the kind of day that only cricket could give, where one story ended and others began.

Acknowledgements and Sources

This book is based on my blog The Old Batsman, which began one Sunday in November 2008. Some parts of the book feature blog posts rewritten and edited to fit the narrative here. In addition, I'd like to thank Matt Thacker at *The Nightwatchman*, Wisden's quarterly journal of cricket writing, for permission to rewrite and reuse the pieces he commissioned on Mark Ramprakash and Tony Shillinglaw. I'd also like to thank ESPN Cricinfo for allowing me to do the same to the pieces on batmaking and Barry Richards that I wrote for them. The idea for *The Meaning of Cricket* was inspired in part by Timothy O'Grady's *On Golf*, a wonderful book, from which I took the liberty of borrowing the idea for the structure of the first chapter.

For research and stats that appear throughout this book, I'd like to acknowledge ESPN Cricinfo [espncricinfo. com], Cricket Archive [cricketarchive.com], and the *Wisden Cricketers' Almanack*.

And the following books and authors, either for the research quoted or for broadening my knowledge and informing the text:

Mike Atherton, *Opening Up* (Hodder)

Mike Atherton, *Glorious Summers and Discontents* (Simon & Schuster)

Charlie Connelly, *Gilbert* (John Wisden)

David Epstein, *The Sports Gene* (Yellow Jersey)

David Frith, *Silence of the Heart* (Mainstream)

Gideon Haigh, *The Green and Golden Age* (Aurum Press)

Nick Hornby, *Fever Pitch* (Gollancz)

Simon Hughes, *A Lot of Hard Yakka* (Headline)

Nasser Hussain, *Playing With Fire* (Michael Joseph)

Simon Jones, *The Test: My Life and the Greatest Ashes Series* (Yellow Jersey)

Leo McKinstry, *Boycs* (Corgi)

John Major, *More than a Game* (Harper Perennial)

Andrew Murtagh, *Sundial in the Shade: The Story of Barry Richards* (Pitch)

John Nyren, *The Cricketers of My Time* (Robson Books)

Timothy O'Grady, *On Golf* (Yellow Jersey)

Ricky Ponting, *At the Close of Play* (HarperCollins)

Simon Rae, *W. G. Grace* (Faber and Faber)

Jonathan Rendall, *Twelve Grand* (Yellow Jersey)

Barry Richards, *The Barry Richards Story* (Faber and Faber)

Peter Roebuck, *It Never Rains* (Allen & Unwin)

Peter Roebuck, *Tangled Up In White* (Hodder & Stoughton)

Tony Shillinglaw and Brian Hale, *Bradman Revisited* (Parrs Wood Press)

Richard Tomlinson, *Amazing Grace: The Man Who Was WG* (Little, Brown)

Robert Winder, *The Little Wonder* (Bloomsbury)

Nicholas Wanostrocht, *Felix on the Bat* (Forgotten Books)
Steve Waugh, *Out of My Comfort Zone* (Penguin Books)
Bob Woolmer, Tim Noakes and Helen Moffett, *Bob Woolmer's Art and Science of Cricket* (New Holland)

Also the following articles:
'It Took 10 Years to Recover: The Story of Scott Boswell and the Yips', Andy Bull, *Guardian*
'The Man to Watch Is Prince Inzamam', Mike Selvey, *Guardian*
'Bluey the Indomitable', David Hopps, ESPN Cricinfo
'The Unforgiven', Siddhartha Vaidyanathan, ESPN Cricinfo
'Jeff Thomson Is Annoyed', Christian Ryan, *Wisden Cricketers' Almanack*/ESPN Cricinfo
'Peter Roebuck Was a Brilliant Writer and Brave Batsman, But He Was Never Destined to Live an Easy Life', Derek Pringle, *Daily Telegraph*
'Peter Roebuck: A Gifted Writer and a Complex Man', Vic Marks, *Observer*
'The Devil and José Mourinho', Jonathan Wilson, *The Blizzard*

Thanks to everyone I've played cricket with and against, especially my early team-mates at Fleet CC, Wrecclesham CC and Basingstoke & North Hants CC, and those at Gover Cricket School, especially Jim Cameron, Alf Gover, John Gover, Terry the barman. And to my current team-mates, who I probably won't get shot of now: Charlie the skipper, Hoggy, Big Tone aka Lasers, The Lion, Jammo, Bearders, Biggles, Alehouse, Roomie, Shamso, Wilson

Wilson, Basher, Preggers, Narco, Matthew Parker, Sleevo, Waheed, Diggy, Tristan Jones, Chadders, Daniel Rosenthal, Rhino, Amol, Laura The Scorer, Will Sutton, Zaltz, Ollie C, Jonathan Beckman and those still to come.

And also: Sam Collins, Jarrod Kimber; Phil Walker, Jo Harmon and everyone at All Out Cricket; Charlotte Atyeo; Leslie Matthew, Osman Samiuddin and all at ESPN Cricinfo.

My agent Lucy Luck, and Matt Phillips, Fran Jessop and Tim Broughton at Yellow Jersey.

And especially to my family: Lily Hotten, Ruby Hotten, Yasmin Hounsell, Julie Simpson, Caroline Cope, Keith Mason, and my mum and dad, to whom this book is dedicated.

penguin.co.uk/vintage